Anonymus

Report of President of Queen's College

Belfast, 1895-96

Anonymus

Report of President of Queen's College
Belfast, 1895-96

ISBN/EAN: 9783742811035

Manufactured in Europe, USA, Canada, Australia, Japa

Cover: Foto ©Suzi / pixelio.de

Manufactured and distributed by brebook publishing software
(www.brebook.com)

Anonymus

Report of President of Queen's College

THE REPORT

OF THE

PRESIDENT

OF

QUEEN'S COLLEGE, BELFAST,

FOR

THE SESSION 1895-96.

Presented to both Houses of Parliament by Command of Her Majesty.

DUBLIN:
PRINTED FOR HER MAJESTY'S STATIONERY OFFICE,
BY ALEXANDER THOM & CO. (LIMITED).

And to be purchased, either directly or through any Bookseller, from
HODGES, FIGGIS & Co. (LIMITED), 104, Grafton-street, Dublin; or
EYRE AND SPOTTISWOODE, East Harding-street, Fleet-street, E.C. ; or
JOHN MENZIES & Co., 12, Hanover-street, Edinburgh, and
90, West Nile-street, Glasgow.

1896.

THE REPORT

OF THE

PRESIDENT OF QUEEN'S COLLEGE, BELFAST,

FOR THE

YEAR 1895-96.

TO THE QUEEN'S MOST EXCELLENT MAJESTY.

MAY IT PLEASE YOUR MAJESTY,

I have the honour to present to Your Majesty my annual Report on the condition and progress of Queen's College, Belfast, during the academic year 1895-96. The following are—

THE STATISTICS OF THE YEAR.

The number of students in attendance was 392, being an increase of 6 on the previous year. Of these 355 were matriculated students, and 37 non-matriculated; whereas in 1894-95 only 340 were matriculated and 46 were not. The numbers in the several Faculties were—Faculty of Arts, 139; Faculty of Medicine, 228; Faculty of Law, 23; School of Engineering, 8. These numbers added together make 398, but as 6 students attended in more than one Faculty, the true total is that stated above, viz., 392.

It is interesting to compare these figures with those of the first year of the history of the College. Then only 90 matriculated students were in attendance, as against the 355 now reported, while 105 had passed no matriculation examination. Three years later the College had only 154 students altogether, matriculated and non-matriculated, on its books. Since that time there have been, owing to various causes, many fluctuations in the attendance, but the comparison which I have made between the day of small things of fifty years ago and the attendance of the year just ended is instructive and reassuring.

The large majority of the students last session came, as usual, from Belfast and the various districts of Ulster. The three other Provinces of Ireland were, however, also represented, and we had, in addition, students from England, Scotland, Spain, France, the United States of America, Canada, Bermuda, British Guiana, Australia, India, Ceylon, Syria, Japan, and Cape Colony. Two hundred and forty-three were over twenty-one years of age, and one hundred and forty-nine younger. As usual, all the religious denominations which prevail in the North of Ireland were represented, the College being open to all classes of Your Majesty's subjects, without any distinction whatsoever.

A 2

THE ADMISSION OF WOMEN.

Among those attending College during the year were seventeen young ladies—the largest number that we have yet had in any session. In my last report, after stating the number of ladies that had been enrolled, I said—"No doubt many more of them would attend, were it not that, in the opinion of the Law Officers of the Crown in Ireland, our scholarships and prizes are not open to them. From this disability I sincerely hope they will soon be relieved." It gives me pleasure now to be able to chronicle the fact that the relief thus hoped for has come. By a warrant under Your Majesty's Royal Sign Manual, dated 4th December, 1895, certain alterations and additions have been made in the statutes of the College, and one of the latter is as follows :—"All Scholarships and Prizes shall be open to students of either sex." These amended statutes will come into operation on 1st October next, and therefore at the examinations for scholarships which will be held in the course of that month, women will be admissible. Counsel's opinion has been taken as to whether the scholarships, studentships, &c., which have been founded in the College by private endowment are also now to be open to either sex. A reply in the affirmative has been received. The competition for our various honours, always keen and healthy, may therefore be expected to prove unusually interesting next session, owing to this wider opening of our doors. The importance of the encouragement and assistance which will be given to the higher education of women by the placing at their disposal of studentships, scholarships, and other prizes of various kinds, of the annual value in all of over £2,000, can scarcely be exaggerated.

Now that the question of the admission of women to all the benefits of the College has thus been settled, it may be well to place its history succinctly on record. Originally the institution was only open to men. In 1881 women were admitted to the classes in the Faculty of Arts, but the opinion of the Law Officers, already referred to, debarred them from the enjoyment of any Scholarship or Prize, and indeed also from the legal status of students. In 1889 the further step was taken of allowing them to attend lectures in the Faculty of Medicine, and, later on, all the College classes in all the Faculties were open to them, but still only in the restricted sense imposed by the existing statutes. Now, in 1896, the final stage has been reached, and all barriers have disappeared from their path. It will be noticed that the College has proceeded with due caution and deliberation in making this important change, each forward step having only been taken as experience warranted, and not until it was plainly seen that no evil results, but on the contrary much good, had followed the initial efforts, was the final step resolved upon to which Your Majesty's gracious sanction has now been given—a step which will, I trust, result in large benefit to the higher education of the North of Ireland.

THE DISCIPLINE OF THE COLLEGE.

I have again the sincere satisfaction of reporting that not a single case of offence against College discipline by any student was brought under the notice of the Council during the past year. This fact speaks for itself. To the honour of the students it must be said that their general behaviour is such as to afford the highest satisfaction to the College authorities, and to render the task of maintaining due discipline within our walls pleasantly easy.

THE DEATH-ROLL OF THE YEAR.

I am happy to be able to report to Your Majesty that no breach was made in the ranks of our staff during the year. We had to lament, however, the death of a former Professor who, for the thirty-three years from 1857 to 1890, occupied an honoured place among us, and held also deservedly high rank as a physician of rare skill and ability not only in Belfast but all over Ulster. I refer to Dr. James Seaton Reid, late Professor of Materia Medica, whose mortal remains were in May last followed to their last resting place in the City cemetery by a large body of mourners, representative both of the City and the College.

Nor can I help alluding to another death which occurred during the year, although it was not that of one of our number. By the demise of the late Sir E. J. Harland, Bart., M.P., the College undoubtedly lost one of its best and ablest friends, one who recognised, as few men have done, the immense importance to this city and the entire country of maintaining it in the fullest efficiency, and who, from the time of his election as a member of the Imperial Parliament, gave me readily and heartily the most valuable aid from time to time in obtaining for it from the State the recognition and assistance which it required.

We had to lament also losses among our graduates. One of these was specially deplored in the College, that of Dr. John Strahan, who, though his sun may be said to have gone down while it was yet day, had deservedly gained a singularly high reputation for his knowledge of medicine, and whose death brought mourning into many a household where he had proved himself not merely the skilled physician but the trusted friend. His essay on "The Fevers of the United Kingdom" gained the Fothergill Gold Medal of the Medical Society of London in 1886, and his treatise on "The Diagnosis and Treatment of Extra-Uterine Pregnancy" the Jenks Prize of the College of Physicians, Philadelphia, in 1880.

ADDITIONS TO THE STAFF.

Two additional lectureships have, with the sanction of His Excellency the Lord Lieutenant of Ireland, been founded during the year, one in Ophthalmology and Otology, and one in Sanitary Science. To the former Dr. W. A. M'Keown, an *alumnus* of the College, whose eminence as an oculist is well known all over the medical world, has been appointed. The latter has been placed in the joint charge of Dr. E. A. Letts, Professor of Chemistry in the College, who will lecture on those portions of the prescribed course which come within the domain of chemistry, and Dr. Henry Whitaker, Medical Superintendent Medical Officer of Health to the City of Belfast, who will, in virtue of his official position, have special facilities for familiarising his students with the practical details of Sanitary Science.

A class in Bacteriology has also been commenced during the year, with Dr. Lorrain Smith as lecturer. The wisdom of establishing it is proved by the fact that, although a purely voluntary class, it began with a roll of eighteen members.

So many changes of various kinds have of late occurred in the teaching staff that I think it advisable to give here a complete list of its present members. They are as follows:—

The Greek Language,	Professor DILL, M.A.
The Latin Language,	Professor DOUGAN, M.A.
Mathematics,	Professor PURSER, M.A., LL.D., F.R.C.L.
Natural Philosophy,	Professor EVERETT, M.A., D.C.L., F.R.S., F.R.U.L.
History and English Literature,	Professor MACMULLAN, M.A., F.R.U.L.
Logic and Metaphysics,	Professor PARK, M.A., D.LIT, F.R.U.L.
Chemistry,	Professor LETTS, PH.D., F.R.A.S., F.R.U.L.
Natural History and Geology,	Professor CUNNINGHAM, M.D., D.SC., F.L.S., F.G.S., F.R.U.L.
Modern Languages,	Professor METHVEN, PH.D.
Jurisprudence & Political Economy,	Professor GRAHAM, M.A.
English Law,	Professor SHARMAN, M.A., LL.B.
Anatomy,	Professor SYMINGTON, M.D., F.R.S.E., F.R.U.L.
Dunville Chair of Physiology,	Professor THOMPSON, M.D., F.R.C.P., &c.
Medicine,	Professor CUMING, M.A., M.D., F.K.Q.C.P.
Surgery,	Professor SINCLAIR, M.D., M.C.H., F.R.C.S.I., &c.
Materia Medica,	Professor WHITLA, M.D.
Midwifery,	Professor BYERS, M.A., M.D., M.CH.
Civil Engineering,	Professor FITZGERALD, B.A., Assoc. M.I.C.E.
Agriculture,	} Professor HODGES, M.D., F.C.S., F.I.C.
Medical Jurisprudence,	
Pathology,	J. LORRAIN SMITH, M.D.
Ophthalmology and Otology,	W. A. M'KEOWN, M.D.
Sanitary Science,	{ E. A. LETTS, PH.D., F.R.C.S., V.C & Henry Whitaker, M.D.
Practical Pharmacy,	VICTOR G. L. FIELDEN, M.B.

It will be seen from this list that there are at present twenty-four professors and lecturers in the College, not reckoning demonstrators and assistants.

THE HONOURS AND SUCCESSES OF THE YEAR.

From its earliest days Queen's College, Belfast, has been noted for the high positions which its students have taken at the Universities and at other public examinations. I am happy to be able to say that, judging from the latest returns, there appears to be no falling off in this respect. . It would be impossible to record here all the honours which have been won during the year. In the Appendix to this Report I shall furnish a complete list. Here I content myself with mentioning a few of the more striking.

Most of our students resort for their degrees to the Royal University of Ireland, whose examinations are well known to be among the most testing in the United Kingdom. The results of these examinations during the year 1895-96, so far as the honours gained by the students of this College are concerned, may be summarised thus:—At the Summer Examinations of 1895 the Queen's College, Belfast, candidates carried off a total of 19 First Classes and 28 Second Classes in the Faculties of Arts and Medicine, together with 16 Exhibitions varying in value from £42 to £15. At the Autumn Examinations they gained 7 First Classes and 12 Second Classes in the Faculties of Arts, Medicine, Law, and Engineering, with 11 Exhibitions varying in value from £42 to £10. At the same Examinations the Studentship in Mathematics, the pecuniary value of which is £800, was gained by one of our students, Mr. J. G. Leathem. Another, Mr. Robert Magill, was awarded by the Senate a Gold Medal and a Special Prize of £50 for his highly distinguished answering in Mental Science at the Examination for the Degree of M.A. At the Spring Examinations of this year, out of seven candidates for the Degrees of M.B., B.Ch., and B.A.O. who were placed by the Examiners in the Upper Pass division, five were from this College, and two of them were awarded Exhibitions for their distinguished answering.

At other Universities our students have also taken some very high places during the year, a complete list of which will be found in the Appendix to this Report. I may specially mention the following:—At the Mathematical Tripos Examinations in the University of Cambridge in the Summer of this year, Mr. W. A. Houston was bracketed Fifth Wrangler. During the year Mr. R. K. M'Elderry gained a prize in the same University for the best Latin Essay on "England's Sea Power," while Mr. J. G. Leathem was elected to the Sir Isaac Newton Studentship founded for the promotion of research in Astronomy or Physical Optics, the value of which is £200 per annum for three years. At the University of Oxford Mr. D. D. Reid was awarded a First in the Modern History Class List.

Nor have our Law students been behind their compeers in the other Faculties in the honours which they have gained. This summer the Benchers of King's Inns, Dublin, have awarded the first Victoria Prize in the Senior Class to Mr. J. M. Whitaker, and the second to Mr. M. Ellison, while the first prize in the Junior Class was divided between two other men of this College, Mr. Henry Hanna and Mr. Robert Spencer Park, and in the Law Students' Debating Society of King's Inns the David Lynch Silver Medal for Legal Debate was gained by Mr. H. Hanna.

. With the mention of one other victory I close this account. At the examination for County Surveyorships held in last autumn Mr. J. W. Leebody gained the first place among all the candidates. He succeeded in obtaining 770 marks out of the possible total of 1,000. It is unnecessary to say that I have the utmost pleasure in recording this long and brilliant series of distinctions won by our *alumni* during the year—distinctions which evince high ability, and were gained by incessant toil, and which are not only honourable to the fortunate winners, but reflect the greatest credit on their *alma mater*, especially on the Professors under whom they were trained in their several departments of study.

Among distinctions of another kind which have been conferred on *alumni* of the College during the year, the following may be mentioned :—Sir William M'Cormac, M.A., M.D., D.Sc., elected President of the Royal College of Surgeons of England ; Mr. John Perry, M.E., F.R.S., appointed Professor of Mechanics and Mathematics in the Royal College of Science, London ; Rev. Thomas Macafee Hamill, M.A., appointed Professor of Theology in Assembly's College, Belfast ; Rev. George Woodburn, M.A., appointed Professor of English and Logic in Magee College, Londonderry ; and Mr. J. Andrew Strahan, M.A., LL.B., Professor of English Law in this College, elected an Honorary Associate of the Royal Institute of British Architects in recognition of the services he has rendered to the profession by his writings on the law relating to architects, and in other ways. All these honours were heard of among us with lively satisfaction.

ALTERATION OF THE COLLEGE CHARTER.

I have already referred to the alteration of the Charter of the College by Your Majesty in December last in regard to one important particular, viz., the admission of women. Other changes which were also made in it by the Royal Warrant were :—

(1.) The creation of new Scholarships in the Faculty of Medicine to meet the extension of the course for the Degrees of M.B., B.Ch., and B.A.O., from four years, its former length, to five, as now required by the General Medical Council. There are now ten Scholarships in this Faculty.

(2.) The abbreviation of the academic course in Law from three years to two, to harmonize with the requirements of the Benchers of King's Inns and of the Incorporated Law Society.

(3.) A redistribution of the Law Scholarships.

(4.) An alteration of the system under which Second and Third Year Scholarships in the Faculty of Arts have hitherto been awarded, power being now given to the Council to require a separate examination for the Third Year Scholarships—a power which they have resolved to exercise.

These changes have been made at our request, and will come into operation on 1st October next. We trust they will all be found conducive to the greater furtherance of the cause of education in Ireland.

THE REPORTS OF THE DEANS OF RESIDENCES.

I have received the following Reports from the Deans of Residences, whose disinterested labours on behalf of the Students I highly appreciate:—

"St. Andrew's Rectory,

"University Square,

"Belfast, 4th June, 1890.

" DEAR MR. PRESIDENT,—In response to your letter of the 3rd inst., I have to make the following Report of the Church of Ireland students of Queen's College, Belfast, for the past Session. I am again happy in being able to express my conviction that the students have exhibited in their moral conduct almost everything that could be expected. Indeed, I am sure that the whole tone of the College has been for many years gradually and surely developing for greater good. And when the now nearly completed "Union" building is in operation, new opportunities of a valuable character will arise for still greater improvement.

"Much of this advance is caused by the healthful and religious influence of the "Christian Union of Queen's College." This Society not only continues its work, but has succeeded in causing the formation of a Women's Branch to meet the case of a numerously increasing roll of lady students.

"Soon after the opening of the First Term of last winter's Session the Lord Bishop of Down and Connor held a special service, and preached a sermon addressed to students in my Church of St. Andrew. A large number of students attended, and the presence of the President of Queen's College and that of the Registrar (Professor Purser) marked the sympathy of the officials with the young men. I have also made some little efforts towards aiding the students to establish a more intimate bond among them than mere studentship would accomplish.

"With the other Deans, I have to express the hope that in the new "Union Buildings" this "Christian Union" may have such a place as may help its further prosperous development.

"I remain, dear Mr. President,

"Yours very faithfully,

"S. EDWARD BUSBY, Clk., LL.D.,

"Dean (I.C.), Q.C.B."

"3 College Park, Belfast,

"10th June, 1890.

"DEAR MR. PRESIDENT,—I have much pleasure in reporting that, as far as I have been able to learn, the conduct of the students belonging to the Presbyterian Church has been most satisfactory.

"I conducted a weekly Bible Class for young men, to which students were specially invited, and a considerable number of students—about thirty—were members of this class and attended it during the Session.

"I preached a special sermon for students in Rosemary-street Church, at which the middle aisle of the Church was reserved exclusively for Queen's College students, and a large number of them attended the service.

" Meetings of the members of the Students' Christian Union were
regularly held in the College during the Session, and several addresses
on religious subjects were given to them; and I believe that the
members of this Union are exercising a wholesome Christian influence
on their fellow-students.

" I am,

" Yours faithfully,

" MATTHEW LEITCH,

" Presbyterian Dean of Residences."

" 5th June, 1896.

" DEAR MR. PRESIDENT,—Regarding the Methodist Students attending the Queen's College, and under my care as Dean of Residences I
am glad to be able to say that, so far as I know, their conduct during
the past year has been eminently satisfactory. Some of them are
Members of the Students' Christian Union, and exercise a very
beneficial influence over their fellow students.

" I am, very truly yours,

" WM. NICHOLAS, D.D.,

" Methodist Dean of Residences.

" The President,
" Queen's College, Belfast."

" Adelaide Park, Belfast,

" June, 6, 1896.

" DEAR SIR,—I am happy to be able to report favourably of the
Students who have been under my care.

" Yours faithfully,

" DOUGLAS WALMSLEY.

" To the President,
" Queen's College, Belfast."

ADDITIONS TO THE COLLEGE BUILDINGS.

In my last Report I referred with pleasure to the fact that the
erection of a new block of buildings, to be devoted to teaching
and research in Physiology and Pathology, had been commenced.
I am happy to say now that this building has been completed
and already brought partially into use, the departments of Pathology and Bacteriology having been conducted in it during the
summer session of this year. The accommodation afforded by it
comprises lecture-rooms, practical class-rooms, laboratories, cul-
ture-room, &c.—in fact all the rooms necessary for the successful
study of these important and growing sciences. Already the
value of the building has been amply proved, lecturers and
students being alike able to pursue their work in it not only with
greater comfort, but with much more efficiency than was hereto-
fore possible.

The foundation stone of the College Union, which is being erected by means of monies obtained by public subscription, was very kindly laid on 18th January last by His Excellency the Lord Lieutenant of Ireland (The Right Hon. Earl Cadogan, K.G.), and, ever since, the building has been vigorously pushed forward under the superintendence of its accomplished architect, Mr. Robert Cochrane, F.R.I.B.A., Surveyor for the Northern District to the Commissioners of Public Works, and an *alumnus* of this College, to whose skill and attention I cannot but express our obligations here, not only for the beautiful plans which he drew for the Union, and the care with which he has watched over its erection, but for the taste and efficiency with which he has seen to the maintenance of all the College buildings since they came under his charge. It is expected that the Union will be ready for occupation some time in next session. It promises not only to afford most commodious and suitable accommodation for the purposes for which it is intended, but to be also a most elegant and handsome addition to the College buildings. Undoubtedly it will conduce materially to the comfort and well being of the students in attendance at College, and it is hoped that it will also furnish a congenial meeting-place to which former students will frequently resort, not only to enjoy for themselves the advantages which it will afford, but to give the benefit of their presence and experience to those who are commencing academic life.

While speaking of our buildings, I regret to be obliged, even at the risk of seeming importunate, to press once more upon Your Majesty's Government the necessity of providing further additions to the equipment of the College. I shall mention only three of these much needed additions, not because they exhaust the list, but because they stand first, in my opinion, in the order of necessity. They are:—1. A Physical Laboratory. 2. A Biological Laboratory. 3. The completion of the block of buildings devoted to Chemistry by the erection of the lecture theatre originally contemplated, and provided for on the plans drawn by the Board of Works. I feel bound to say that the College suffers severely in more ways than one, and Professors and students endure much inconvenience, because of the want of the three buildings to which I here refer. Physical Laboratory, strange to say, we have none, save such as can be roughly improvised in a lecture room. A Biological Laboratory is also non-existent—the Professor being obliged to utilise for the purpose a corner of the anatomical dissecting room when he can get it. And the inconvenience and loss caused by the delay in completing the chemical buildings, by the erection of the lecture theatre arranged for when they were begun, can only be properly understood by those who have tried the experiment of endeavouring to be in two different places at the same time. Professor, demonstrator, attendants, and students are kept flitting about daily from the old lecture theatre to the new buildings, and back from the new buildings to the old, and not only moving themselves, but taking delicate and easily-injured apparatus along with them. I therefore most earnestly urge the immediate provision of these three requisite additions. Now that the people of Belfast are manifesting a laudable interest in the affairs of the College—an interest which will, I hope, increase from year to year with the increase of the city and our ever-growing needs— I trust that the State will extend a judicious encouragement to the exercise of local beneficence by dealing in a liberal spirit with such necessities as I have now mentioned. So long as the College is connected with the State, by which it was founded, the State has a duty to discharge towards it, a duty which is laid down in the Colleges Act, and will, I trust, be recognised more clearly and discharged more vigorously as the years roll on; and, on the other hand, as has well been said—"The provision of State protection should never be permitted to absorb the self-reliance or to supersede the self-action of the community in promoting the education and elevation of the people." Instead of being regarded as a reason for standing aloof from helping the College, State aid should surely rather prove a stimulus and an encouragement to exertion on its behalf.

Our Funds.

I regret also to be obliged to say that the funds which are at the disposal of the College for the support of the various scientific departments are proving so insufficient that these departments are suffering seriously. When it is remembered how enormously science has advanced during the past half century, several sciences having, it may be said, been created within that period, and all having developed very materially, and when the fact is borne in mind that the annual grant for the maintenance of the College has remained at the same figure during all those years, this deficiency ought not to be surprising. Within the last five years alone, five entirely new scientific departments have been established in the College, and several which were previously in existence have been so expanded that they might almost be said to be new also. The additional buildings which have been erected necessitate also additional expenditure. With all the economy which the Council can exercise they have not been able adequately to meet these increasing demands, and yet we recognise that unless we keep pace with the advance of the times our labours must be shorn of much of their usefulness and value. I feel it to be my duty to represent this serious condition of things to Your Majesty, and I trust that measures may be devised for meeting it, so that the good work in which the College is engaged, and which, I take leave to say, it has done and is doing with such remarkable success and at a cost to the public purse so small, may not be hampered or crippled.

Visit of His Excellency the Lord Lieutenant of Ireland.

In January last His Excellency the Lord Lieutenant of Ireland, accompanied by the Countess Cadogan, honoured the College with a visit which was hailed with sincere pleasure. An address from the President and Council was presented to him on the occasion, and also an address from the students. To both His Excellency was pleased to reply in very gracious terms.

THE JUBILEE OF THE COLLEGE.

It is intended to celebrate the completion of the fiftieth year of the life of the College early in the coming year, and arrangements for this purpose are in progress. I am happy to be able to state that the Lord Lieutenant has most kindly and cordially acceded to my request that he would honour us with his presence on the occasion, and I sincerely trust that our *alumni* and the citizens of Belfast will unite with us in worthily marking the completion of the first half century of the life of a seat of learning which is universally acknowledged to have conferred, during its comparatively brief existence, innumerable blessings on our common community.

THE COLLEGE LIBRARY.

During the year there were added to the College Library 664 volumes and 142 other publications, or 806 in all. Most of these were purchased, but for a considerable number we were indebted to the kindness of *alumni* or other friends. A full list of these generous donations is given in an Appendix to this Report, but I must here mention, as deserving of special notice, two valuable gifts, one of fifty volumes treating of philosophical subjects, presented by Professor Park, D.Lit., and another of fifty-five publications on topics connected with agriculture, given by Professor Hodges, M.D. The Library now contains nearly 54,000 volumes, and is by far the largest in Belfast.

The preparation of the new Catalogue, to which I have referred in previous reports, is being steadily carried on under the careful supervision of Dr. Meissner, our accomplished Librarian. The compilation of a work so large, and involving in its progress so many inquiries, cannot be rapidly accomplished, but I cherish the confident expectation that it will be completed at no distant date.

At the commencement of the session a new Library Committee was appointed, which met regularly during the winter and bestowed much attention on the affairs of the Library, to its undoubted advantage.

THE COLLECTION OF COINS.

Nearly forty years ago a commencement was made towards the formation of a collection of Greek and Roman coins for the College. Considerable purchases were made at that time and since. These, however, were never properly catalogued or arranged. At my request David Buick, Esq., M.A., LL.D., an esteemed *alumnus* of the College, and a high authority on numismatics, very kindly undertook this task, which he has now completed. He has furnished me with a detailed report which shows that the collection consists of 294 gold and silver coins, which are distributed thus—Greek series 94, Roman series 100, miscellaneous 1. Dr. Buick has compiled a full catalogue of all—

those of the Greek series being arranged in accordance with the
order adopted in the *Historia Nummorum*, those of the Roman
consular series alphabetically, according to the families to which
they belong, and those of the Roman imperial series in the order
of time. The collection will now be exhibited in cases constructed
for the purpose, and, on behalf of the College, I record here my
thanks to Dr. Buick for this very valuable service which, at the
expense of a good deal of time and trouble, he has rendered to
his *alma mater*.

In the course of the year a movement was organised for the
purpose of having a portrait of the Rev. George Hill, the well-
known author of "The Plantation in Ulster," and "The
MacDonnells of Antrim," who was Librarian from 1850 to 1880,
painted for the College. At a meeting held in December last
the following Committee was appointed for this purpose :—

The President of Queen's College (Rev. Thomas Hamilton, D.D.,
LL.D.), Chairman.

The Lord Mayor of Belfast (W. J. Pirrie, Esq., J.P.)

The Master of the Rolls in Ireland.	J. J. Austin, M.D.
Lord Macnaghten.	Sir William MacCormac, M.D.
Sir F. E. Macnaghten.	Professor Purser, LL.D.
The Rev. G. Raphael Buick,	Professor Park, D.LIT.
LL D. (Moderator of the	Professor Dill, M.A.
General Assembly).	Lavens M. Ewart, J.P.
The Rev. R. W. Seaver, M.A.	W. H. Patterson.
The Rev. Charles Scott, M.A.	Richard Lilburn.
The Rev. W. Todd Martin, D.LIT.	John Vinycomb.
The Rev. Alex. Gordon, M.A.	R. M. Young, B.A., J.P.
Professor Redfern, M.D.	John M'Bride.
J. A. Lindsay, M.D.	James A. M'Neill, B.A.
Professor Cuming, M.D.	Robert Dods, B.A.

William Swanston, Treasurer.

Professor Meissner and Francis Joseph Bigger, Secretaries.

Subscriptions at once flowed in. The painting of the portrait
was entrusted to Mr. H. R. Douglas, and it is hoped that it will be
hung early in the ensuing session.

THE MUSEUMS AND LABORATORIES.

All the Museums and Laboratories have been well maintained
during the year. A considerable number of valuable specimens
have been purchased for the Natural History Museum, which
has also been enriched by several presentations. Among these
prominence must be given to one received from Hugh Hyndman,
Esq., LL.D., a well known *alumnus* of the College. It consists
of a collection of Irish plants and other specimens made by
his uncle, the late George C. Hyndman, Esq., who was well known
in his day as one of the highest authorities on our local fauna and
flora. Several important presentations were also made to the
Medical Museums, the re-arrangement and cataloguing of which
are in progress under the care of the Curator, Professor
Symington.

THE STUDENTS' SOCIETIES.

It has been very gratifying to me during the year to notice the prosperity and activity of the various Students' Societies. The Literary and Scientific Society, under the presidency of Mr. R. H. Ashmore, B.A., and the Medical Students' Association under that of Mr. S. M. Magowan, M.B., had excellent meetings and able discussions.

THE EXTENSION OF UNIVERSITY TEACHING.

Although our local scheme for the Extension of University Teaching is not officially connected with the College, yet, as it is carried out on University lines by University men, most of whom are our *alumni*, and as many of its lectures are given in the College, I may here briefly summarise its proceedings during the past session. The classes which were held were in the following subjects:—Astronomy, Electricity and its Practical Applications, Physiology, Tennyson and the "In Memoriam," and Early English History and Literature, the respective lecturers being Dr. J. L. Dreyer, Astronomer of Armagh Observatory; Mr. W. B. Morton, M.A., Junior Fellow R.U.I.; Professor Thompson, M.D.; the Rev. Samuel M'Comb, B.D.; and the Rev. E. L. Fripp, M.A. The introductory address at the commencement of the Session was given by Professor Dowden, Dublin, who took "John Milton" as his theme, and the closing lecture by "Ian Maclaren" (the Rev. John Watson, D.D.), who discoursed on "Robert Burns, the Poet of the People." An examination was held at the close of each class, at which medals and certificates were awarded. I am glad to say that the work of the Society was well and vigorously done during the session, and I cannot but think that it supplies a felt want among us, and renders a service to the cause of education which could not otherwise be easily supplied.

GRANT FROM THE SORELLA TRUSTEES.

I have the pleasure of reporting that the Sorella Trustees, established under the will of the late William Dunville, Esq., made in the course of the year a grant of £100 towards the purchase of additional apparatus for the department of Physiology—a benefaction which, I need scarcely say, was very thankfully received.

SCIENCE RESEARCH SCHOLARSHIP.

I have just received intimation that Her Majesty's Commissioners for the Exhibition of 1851 have resolved to place the nomination to a Science Research Scholarship of the annual value of £150 at the disposal of the College next year. The intention of the Scholarship is to enable students who have passed through the College curriculum, and have given evidence of capacity for original research, to continue the prosecution of science with the view of aiding its advance or its application to the industries of the country. This is the fourth time that the Commissioners have given us the nomination to one of these very important and valuable Scholarships.

LECTURES.

The Council have had under consideration during the year the advisability of commencing lectures earlier in the Session than hitherto. The various University and College Examinations which fall to be held in September and October render it impossible to do much in this direction. But in the coming Session it has been arranged that lectures in Medicine shall commence on Tuesday, October 20th, and lectures in Arts and Engineering on Monday, November 2nd. Lectures in Law will begin on Wednesday, January 6, 1897.

CONCLUSION.

I have thus briefly sketched the history of the College during the past year. I hope that the account which I have given, short as it necessarily is, is sufficient to show that it continues to serve earnestly and not unsuccessfully the great purposes for which it was founded by Your Majesty, as these are defined in our Charter, viz., "to afford to all classes and denominations of our faithful subjects, without any distinction of religious creed whatsoever, an opportunity for pursuing a regular and liberal course of education." If it was deemed advisable fifty years ago to establish such a College in Belfast, when the population of the city was but 80,000 or 90,000, how much more is such a seat of learning essential now, when the town of those days has grown into a city of about 800,000 inhabitants, and when the port of Belfast, judged by its customs revenue, ranks third in the entire United Kingdom. Along with the liberal support of the State, I trust it will receive from the citizens of Belfast a continually increasing measure of such generous help as similar seats of learning in England and Scotland receive from the cities in which they are situated. Every one knows what Edinburgh and Glasgow and Liverpool and Manchester have done and are continuing to do for their Colleges. It is largely owing to the princely liberality which has been lavished upon them by wealthy and public-spirited citizens that they are what they are to-day. One cannot visit their splendid buildings or scan the long list of the gifts which they have received without longing for the time when Belfast College shall, through like munificence, enjoy a similar position of wealth and usefulness. Our roll of benefactors has already inscribed upon it the names of men whose donations or bequests not only worthily perpetuate their memory, but year by year continually serve the public good. The names of Pakenham and Sullivan and Porter and Dunville and Drennan and Tennent and M'Kane will thus ever be held in grateful remembrance among us. I trust that this honourable list will grow. In not a few departments the College needs, and would gladly welcome, the aid of those who are interested in the educational advancement of Belfast and the North of Ireland, and, as has well been said recently—

"There never was a time when it was more requisite, more urgently necessary, that the principle of mental cultivation should be thrust into the foreground and held up on high before the entire community, for we live in a period when what I may call wealth-making conditions are multiplied to an enormous extent. The enjoyments of life and the conveniences of life have grown around us in a degree that can hardly be conceived by those who have not witnessed the change. The meaning of all this is that wealth is acquiring a still greater hold upon us. Wealth is a good servant but a bad master, and there is no master who has had the power of degrading the human being more than the unchecked dominance of wealth. Against the dominance of wealth a University represents the antagonism which is offered to it by mental cultivation. The mind of man should be treated as a rich domain, requiring only to be well ploughed and to be well sown in order to yield richest harvest, and in order to maintain effectual protest against that unchecked pursuit of material interests which constitutes one of the greatest social, and I may even say one of the greatest spiritual, dangers of the period in which we live."

In the Appendix to this Report I have placed lists of the Visitors, the President, the Professors, the Deans of Residences, and other Officials of the College, together with a series of tables showing (1) the Number of Students matriculated in the Session 1895–96; (2) the Numbers and Religious Persuasions of the Students who have entered in each year since the opening of the College, and the Numbers and Religious Persuasions of the Students who have attended in each year; (3) the Numbers attending in each Faculty during the Session now ended; (4) the Number of Students who came to the College from each of the provinces of Ireland, and from other places, during the Session; (5) the Ages of the Students in attendance; (6) the Number of Lectures given by each Professor during the Session, and the Number of Students attending each Class; (7) the names of the College Scholars and Prizemen for last Session; (8) a list of Degrees, Diplomas, and Honours obtained by Students of the College at the Examinations of the Royal University of Ireland in 1895; (9) a list of sundry Students who have, since 1st January, 1891, obtained distinctions in Universities other than the Royal University of Ireland; (10) a Table showing the Length of Service, Salaries and other Emoluments of the Professors and Officers of the College; (11) a List of the Benefactors of the College since its foundation, with an account of their benefactions; and (12) an account of the Receipts and Expenditure of the College during the year ending 31st March, 1896.

All which is testified on behalf of the College by

Your Majesty's

Most dutiful servant,

THOMAS HAMILTON,

PRESIDENT.

July, 1896.

B

VISITORS.

The Most Honourable the Marquess of Dufferin and Ava, K.P., G.C.B.
The Most Honourable the Marquess of Londonderry, K.G.
The Right Honourable le John Thomas Ball, LL.D.
The Right Honourable A. M. Porter, Master of the Rolls in Ireland.
His Honour Judge Shaw, Q.C.
The Right Rev. Bishop Welland, D.D.
The Right Honourable Thomas Sinclair, P.P., D.L.
The Right Honourable the Chief Secretary for Ireland, for the time being.
The Moderator of the General Assembly of the Presbyterian Church in Ireland, for the time being.
The President of the King's and Queen's College of Physicians, for the time being.
The President of the Royal College of Surgeons, for the time being.
The President of the Association of Non-Subscribing Presbyterians of Ireland for the time being.

PRESIDENT, PROFESSORS, OFFICERS, AND DEANS OF RESIDENCES.

President.

THE REV. THOMAS HAMILTON, M.A., D.D., LL.D.

Professors.

The Greek Language,	SAMUEL DILL, M.A.
The Latin Language.	THOMAS WILSON DOUGAN, M.A.
Mathematics,	JOHN PURSER, LL.D., F.R.U.I.
Natural Philosophy,	JOSEPH DAVID EVERETT, M.A., D.C.L., F.R.S., F.R.U.I.
History and English Literature,	SAMUEL J. MACMULLAN. M.A. F.R.U.I.
Logic and Metaphysics,	JOHN PARK, M.A., D.LIT., F.R.U.I.
Chemistry,	EDMUND A. LETTS, PH.D., F.R.S., F.C.S., F.R.U.I.
Natural History and Geology,	ROBERT O. CUNNINGHAM, M.D., D.SC., F.L.S., F.G.S., C.M.Z.S., F.R.U.I.
Modern Languages.	ALBERT L. MEISSNER, PH.D.
Jurisprudence & Political Economy,	WILLIAM GRAHAM, M.A.
English Law,	JAMES A. STRAHAN, M.A., LL.B.
Anatomy,	JOHNSON SYMINGTON, M.D., F.R.S.R., F.R.C.S.I.
Physiology,	WILLIAM HENRY THOMPSON, M.D., F.R.C.S.I.
Medicine.	JAMES CUMING, M.A., M.D., F.R.Q.C.P.
Surgery,	THOMAS SINCLAIR, M.D., M.CH., F.R.C.S., Esq.
Materia Medica,	WILLIAM WHITLA, M.D.
Midwifery,	JOHN W. BYERS, M.D.
Civil Engineering,	MAURICE F. FITZGERALD, B.A., ASSOC. M.I.C.E.
Agriculture,	JOHN F. HODGES, M.D., F.C.S., F.I.C.

Lecturers.

Medical Jurisprudence,	JOHN F. HODGES, M.D., F.C.S., F.I.C.
Pathology,	J. LORRAIN SMITH, M.A., M.D.

Demonstrator.

Practical Pharmacy,	VICTOR G. L. FIELDEN, M.B.

Office Bearers.

Registrar,	JOHN PURSER, LL.D.
Bursar,	WILLIAM WYLIE, ESQ.
Librarian,	A. L. MEISSNER, PH.D.

Curator of Natural History Museum.
PROFESSOR CUNNINGHAM, M.D.

Curator of Medical Museum.
PROFESSOR SYMINGTON, M.D.

Deans of Residences.

		Appointed
Church of Ireland,	REV. S. EDWARD BOMET, M.A., LL.D.	1872
Presbyterian Church in Ireland,	REV. MATTHEW LEITCH, D.P., D.LIT.	1892
Wesleyan Methodists.	REV. WILLIAM NICHOLAS, D.D.	1895
Association of Irish Non-Subscribing Presbyterians,	REV. DOUGLAS WALMSLEY, B.A.	1895

APPENDIX.

TABLE I.

NUMBER of STUDENTS Matriculated in Session 1895–96 :—

Admitted and examined, having Matriculated in the Royal University,   .   .   29

TABLE II.

A.—NUMBERS and RELIGIOUS PERSUASIONS of STUDENTS who have entered the COLLEGE in each year since its opening.

Sessions.	Matriculated.	Non-Matriculated.	Total.	Presbyterians.	Church of Ireland.	Roman Catholics.	Methodist.	Various.	Total.
1849–50,	90	105	195	145	23	3	4	9	184
1850–51,	51	43	93	43	16	7	1	12	83
1851–52,	43	49	92	47	25	7	3	1	83
1852–53,	31	22	53	24	10	7	2	1	44
1853–54,	39	73	62	30	14	5	3	4	63
1854–55,	41	32	73	44	18	6	3	2	73
1855–56,	33	30	67	24	17	5	3	3	84
1856–57,	39	30	63	49	13	4	1	5	62
1857–58,	45	26	71	45	3	6	9	—	71
1858–59,	51	37	88	31	24	8	4	1	89
Entered in first 10 years,	**461**	**523**	**854**	**573**	**163**	**58**	**23**	**36**	**854**
1859–60,	66	34	90	84	14	6	4	2	90
1860–61,	96	41	107	85	29	13	3	7	107
1861–62,	114	35	183	101	37	5	6	10	138
1862–63,	113	23	187	83	25	12	3	5	107
1863–64,	109	18	107	83	26	5	2	3	127
1864–65,	108	27	135	87	29	6	3	7	134
1865–66,	84	30	116	72	17	7	5	6	116
1866–67,	83	12	107	61	18	6	10	7	107
1867–68,	96	23	119	63	40	5	1	23	119
1868–69,	78	24	103	63	14	7	6	16	103
Entered in second 10 years,	**955**	**260**	**1,215**	**797**	**239**	**73**	**45**	**36**	**1,215**
1869–70,	83	16	99	54	23	3	4	9	98
1870–71,	84	30	114	57	28	9	8	11	114
1871–72,	78	25	103	60	30	6	5	14	105
1872–73,	89	14	113	63	25	6	9	5	113
1873–74,	98	25	123	63	23	5	13	13	123
1874–75,	102	39	134	73	33	3	5	16	134
1875–76,	91	21	113	63	16	10	7	11	115
1876–77,	119	72	161	93	35	3	8	13	151
1877–78,	115	26	141	70	64	10	8	16	141
1878–79,	123	33	141	64	66	10	7	8	146
Entered in third 10 years,	**995**	**267**	**1,262**	**654**	**364**	**64**	**73**	**113**	**1,262**

A.—Numbers and Religious Persuasions of Students who
have entered the College in each year since its opening—
continued.

Sessions.	Matriculated.	Non-Matriculated.	Total.	Presbyterian.	Church of Ireland.	Roman Catholic.	Methodist.	Various.	Total.
1878–79,	128	23	151	90	29	10	10	12	151
1879–81,	135	15	150	91	80	8	4	17	150
1881–82,	171	15	188	110	23	11	17	20	188
1882–83,	107	23	130	75	25	5	5	17	130
1883–84,	117	16	185	82	23	6	9	16	133
1884–85,	110	21	131	92	20	2	7	10	171
1885–86,	104	77	181	79	23	8	10	10	151
1886–87,	87	23	110	79	17	–	10	4	110
1887–88,	94	15	109	76	20	3	6	4	102
1888–89,	108	20	129	89	23	8	–	5	126
Entered in fourth 10 years,	1,150	186	1,337	863	237	59	61	118	1,357
1889–90,	142	28	170	104	30	6	13	15	170
1890–91,	110	17	127	87	23	5	6	6	127
1891–92,	139	19	155	107	25	7	11	10	155
1892–93,	89	8	97	62	15	6	4	4	97
1893–94,	83	29	112	83	14	10	10	5	112
1894–95,	92	25	117	79	24	7	7	7	117
1895–96,	99	13	112	74	24	6	8	5	112
Total,	4,526	1,345	5,571	3,453	1,098	301	281	408	5,571

B.—Numbers and Religious Persuasions of Students attending the College in each Session from its opening.

Sessions.	Matriculated.	Non-Matriculated.	Total.	Presbyterians.	Church of Ireland.	Roman Catholic.	Methodist.	Various.	Total.
1849–50,	90	105	195	145	35	5	4	9	195
1850–51,	110	75	185	150	33	10	4	2	185
1851–52,	120	69	189	129	40	14	5	1	189
1852–53,	101	55	154	100	53	15	2	2	154
1853–54,	114	54	168	107	38	14	6	3	168
1854–55,	115	55	183	161	34	14	3	1	183
1855–56,	119	74	193	181	22	19	5	5	193
1856–57,	136	56	194	131	35	14	8	11	194
1857–58,	153	54	207	154	31	14	4	4	207
1858–59,	160	63	223	158	43	14	6	3	223
Average of first 10 years,	172·1	67·0	189·1	131·7	35·3	13·3	4·9	4·2	189·1
1859–60,	199	58	257	184	43	16	8	6	257
1860–61,	239	73	312	216	57	22	7	10	319
1861–62,	299	76	375	266	38	17	11	20	375
1862–63,	332	55	388	278	51	24	11	17	382
1863–64,	340	47	387	261	63	26	10	27	387
1864–65,	356	49	405	285	58	23	9	31	405
1865–66,	360	55	415	281	60	19	13	40	413
1866–67,	557	80	637	723	57	19	16	68	637
1867–68,	857	53	390	235	59	16	24	57	390
1868–69,	330	19	349	220	11	15	24	56	362
Average of second 10 years,	317·5	51·0	368·2	244·6	54·6	19·4	14·4	33·2	368·3

B.—NUMBERS and RELIGIOUS PERSUASIONS of STUDENTS attending the COLLEGE, in each Session from its opening—con.

Sessions.	Matriculated	Non-Matriculated	Total	Presbyterian	Church of Ireland	Roman Catholics	Methodist	Various	Total
1869-70,	328	23	353	214	57	18	10	45	353
1870-71,	327	43	370	226	76	14	21	43	370
1871-72,	335	20	355	239	49	17	18	44	355
1872-73,	320	23	341	203	79	15	21	23	341
1873-74,	344	31	375	201	87	17	20	44	375
1874-75,	348	47	393	229	65	11	21	30	393
1875-76,	348	40	388	237	70	17	29	35	388
1876-77,	393	44	437	270	86	13	29	39	437
1877-78,	421	43	443	303	86	28	27	44	443
1878-79,	443	47	500	259	09	30	33	19	500
Average of third 10 years,	362·9	37·5	400·3	236·5	79·8	16·3	24·2	43·6	400·3
1879-80,	456	38	494	291	63	23	38	34	494
1880-81,	429	36	549	320	90	23	32	48	549
1881-82,	341	26	567	343	104	35	30	55	567
1882-83,	472	20	502	293	91	20	33	53	502
1883-84,	456	25	491	289	85	17	34	55	491
1884-85,	418	21	449	299	81	10	35	44	449
1885-86,	416	44	460	303	66	17	24	47	460
1886-87,	357	38	429	301	81	9	33	35	429
1887-88,	339	31	420	290	64	18	30	39	420
1888-89,	501	31	522	303	89	11	30	27	522
Average fourth 10 years,	441·8	31·7	473·5	304·1	79·4	18·6	30·6	43·9	473·5
1889-90,	411	30	441	287	74	16	27	37	441
1890-91,	403	47	450	299	69	17	27	39	450
1891-92,	445	41	491	323	87	20	33	39	491
1892-93,	414	39	453	340	58	16	39	51	453
1893-94,	550	45	450	303	60	29	19	25	450
1894-95,	540	44	584	345	83	91	37	23	584
1895-96,	525	27	552	324	63	10	15	21	552

TABLE III.

NUMBER of STUDENTS attending each Faculty in Session 1895-96.

Arts, ...	139
Law, ...	23
Medicine, ...	226
Engineering, ...	8
	596
Attending in more than one Faculty, . . .	6
	392

TABLE IV.

NUMBER of STUDENTS who came from each of the PROVINCES of IRELAND, and from other Places.

Ulster, ...	388	United States, . . .	8
Munster, ...	8	Canada, . . .	1
Leinster, ...	10	Japan, . . .	1
Connaught, . . .	3	Bermuda, . . .	
England, . . .	9	British Guiana, . .	1
Scotland, . . .	7	Cape Colony, . .	1
Spain, . . .	3	Syria, . . .	1
India, . . .	3	France, . . .	1
Ceylon, . . .	1		
Australia, . . .	1	Total, . .	392

TABLE V.

AGES of STUDENTS in ATTENDANCE.

Under Seventeen years, ...	3
From Seventeen to Eighteen, ...	13
From Eighteen to Nineteen, ...	28
From Nineteen to Twenty, ...	54
From Twenty to Twenty-one, ...	81
Above Twenty-one years, ...	243
Total, . . .	892

TABLE VI.

NUMBER of LECTURES given by each Professor, and NUMBER of STUDENTS attending them, in Session 1805–90.

—	Number of Lectures	Number of Students
Greek, ...	282*	59
Latin, ...	284†	72
English Language and Literature, . . .	123	46
History, ...	63	10
French, ...	154	86
German, ...	503	9
Logic, ...	108	38
Metaphysics, ...	73	26
Mathematics, ...	236	54
Natural Philosophy, ...	376	130
Chemistry, ...	100	77
Practical Chemistry, Summer, 1895, . .	55	19
Do., Winter, 1895–96, .	65	33
Laboratory, Summer, 1895, .	55	2
Do., Winter, 1895–96, .	394	5
Zoology, ...	57	63
Botany, Summer, 1895, . . .	45	45
Geology and Mineralogy, . . .	38	4
Practical Biology, 2 hours each, Summer, 1896,	35	27
English Law, ...	72	23
Jurisprudence and Civil Law, . .	48	24
Political Economy, . . .	24	19
Anatomy, ...	147	123
Physiology, ...	103	60
Practical Physiology and Histology, each of 2 hours duration, . . .	40	25
Medicine, ...	80	34
Surgery, ...	84	80
Operative Surgery, Summer, 1895, . .	38	27
Midwifery, ...	87	35
Materia Medica, ...	101	62
Medical Jurisprudence, Summer, 1895, .	29	35
Engineering, ...	231	5
Systematic Pathology, Summer, 1895, .	44	29
Practical Pathology, 2 hours each, Summer, 1895,	95	26
Practical Pharmacy, Summer, 1895, .	31	28

* In addition, fifty-six Lectures were given by the Senior Scholar.
† In addition, fifty-nine Lectures were given by the Senior Scholar.
‡ In addition, eighty-one Lectures were given by the Senior Scholar.
§ Days on which the Laboratory was open under the supervision of the Professor.

TABLE VII.
A.—COLLEGE SCHOLARS AND PRIZEMEN.
SESSION 1895-96.

SENIOR SCHOLARS.

GREEK, LATIN, AND ANCIENT HISTORY.
M'Culla, James, B.A.

MODERN LANGUAGES AND MODERN HISTORY.
Wright, Stanley Fowler.

NATURAL PHILOSOPHY.
Makelly, Samuel Shannon, B.A.

LOGIC, METAPHYSICS, AND POLITICAL ECONOMY.
Purvis, Wm. Johnston, B.A. | Simpson, Robert T., B.A.—A prize.

CHEMISTRY.
Brown, John Walter, B.A.

NATURAL HISTORY.
Megaw, John Wallace Dick, B.A. | Adams, John.—A prize.

JUNIOR SCHOLARS.
FACULTY OF ARTS.
Third Year.
####### LITERARY DIVISION.
Lenihan, William Harvey. | Hilton, Robert.
Scott, James Bruce.
Hamill, William D. } equal.
M'Neill, William.

####### SCIENCE DIVISION.
Rice, James. | Dunn, Andrew.
Johnston, James. | Bright, James.

Second Year.
####### LITERARY DIVISION.
Paul, Francis James. | Minford, William.
Armstrong, Frederick William. | Macafee, William.
Porter, Samuel Clarke.

####### SCIENCE DIVISION.
Stoops, William Alex. | Hawthorne, John.
Harvey, Thomas Edwin. | MacGiffin, Henry Alf. } equal.
Stevenson, Howard.

First Year.
####### LITERARY DIVISION.
Peden, Thos. Usher. } equal. | Barr, Andrew.—A prize.
Wilson, George. | Kane, Jas. Whiteford.—A prize.
Sinclair, Wm. Thomas
Jennings, Christian. } equal.
Woods, Robt. Stanton.

####### SCIENCE DIVISION.
Smyth, Samuel Andrew. | M'Crea, Hugh Moreland.
Tombe, Archibald Stuart. | Spence, John Andrew.
Stewart, Samuel Edgar.

FACULTY OF MEDICINE.

Fourth Year.

Anatomy and Physiology.	Therapeutics and Pathology.
M'Cutcheon, Oliver Edward, B.A.	M'Cully, Andrew Lowry.
Hicks, George Adams—A prize.	

Third Year.

M'Master, Arthur Berry.	Henry George Hewitt, B.A.

Second Year.

Rowan, Marriott Logan, B.A.	Thomson, Alfred Mortimer.

First Year.

Ellison, Basil. Charles, literary.	Quinn, James, B.A., science.

FACULTY OF LAW.

Third Year.

M'Cutcheon, Robert Ross, B.A.	Weldon, J. F., B.A., LL.B.—A prize.

Second Year.

Irwin, Alexander, B.A.

First Year.

Barkley, Matthew, B.A.

SCHOOL OF ENGINEERING.

Third Year.

Gailey, Thomas Andrew.

Second Year.

[None.]

First Year.

[None.]

PRIVATE ENDOWMENTS.

DUNVILLE STUDENTSHIP.

Johnstone, Robert James, B.A., elected 1893.

ANDREWS STUDENTSHIP.

Brown, John Walter, B.A., elected 1893.

PORTER SCHOLARSHIPS.

M'Culla, Jas., B.A., elected 1894.	Leatham, W. H., elected 1893.

SULLIVAN SCHOLARSHIPS.

Dunn, Andrew, elected 1893.	Wilson, George, elected 1893.
Stoops, William A., elected 1894.	

REILY, LADY PAKENHAM SCHOLARSHIP.

Heron, Archibald George, elected 1894.

SIR HERCULES PAKENHAM SCHOLARSHIP.

Smyth, Thomas Watt, elected 1895.

BLAYNEY EXHIBITION.

M'Culla, James, B.A., elected 1894.

M'KANE MEDAL.

Barkley, Matthew, B.A.

CLASS PRIZEMEN.

GREEK.

Honour Class.

Leathem, William H. | M'Neill, William.

Second Year.

Paul, F. J. | Armstrong, F. W. } equal
| Porter, S. C.

First Year.

Sinclair, W. T. | Jennings, Christian.

LATIN.

Honour Class
Leathem, W. H.

Second Year.

Armstrong, F. W. | Paul, F. J.
Porter, S. C.

First Year.

Woods, James. | Spence, J. A.
Sinclair, W. T. | Jennings, Christian.

HISTORY.

M'Cullough, A. A. | London, Thomas.

ENGLISH LANGUAGE AND LITERATURE.

Second Year.

Armstrong, F. W. } equal | Harvey, T. R. } equal
Paul, F. J. | Porter, S. C.

First Year.

Phillips, Walter. } equal | Spence, J. A.
Smyth, S. A. | Shannon, Robert.

FRENCH.

Third Year.
Connolly, A. W.

Second Year.
Armstrong, F. W.
Harvey, T. R. } equal
Robinson, W. J.

First Year.

Smyth, T. W. } equal | Phillips, Walter.
Woods, James.

GERMAN.

Third Year.
Connolly, A. W.

Second Year.
Hawthorne, John.

First Year.
Smyth, S. A.

MATHEMATICS.

Honour Class.

Rice, James.

Second Year.

Harvey, T. E.	Stoops, W. A.

First Year.

Tombe, A. S.	Smyth, S. A.
Stewart, S. E.	Spence, J. A.

MATHEMATICAL PHYSICS.

Honour Class.

Orr, W. B.

Second Year.

Harvey, T. E.

EXPERIMENTAL PHYSICS.

Honour Class.

Rice, James.

First Year Arts.

Smyth, S. A.	Armstrong, John.
Spence, J. A.	Stewart, S E.
Phillips, Walter.	

First Year Medical.

Stoops, W. A.	M'Crea, John, B.A.

First Year Engineering.

Galway, J. C.

LOGIC.

Honour Class.

Dunn, Andrew.	Culbert, T. E.

Second Year.

Paul, F. J.	Macafee, William.
Hamilton, S. J.	

METAPHYSICS.

Park, R. J. M.	Culbert, T E.
Dunn, Andrew.	

POLITICAL ECONOMY.

Allen, David.	} equal		Lewis, W. J.
Dunn, Andrew			

GEOLOGY.

Galley, T. A.

ENGINEERING.

Third Year.

Galley, T. A.

First Year.

Galway, J. O.

SYSTEMATIC ANATOMY.

Seniors.

M'Master, A. B.

Juniors, Division A.

Clements, J. E.	M'Mordie, David.

Juniors, Division B.

[Crawford, Annie H.]	West, J. W.

PRACTICAL ANATOMY.

Seniors.

M'Master, A. B.

Second Year.

[Crawford, Annie H.]
Hunter, W. M.
[Huston, Alexandrina C.] } equal.

First Year.

M'Mordie, David.	Clements, J. F.

PHYSIOLOGY AND HISTOLOGY.

Senior Division.

Graham, R. A. L.	M'Cay, David.

Junior Division.

Hunter, W. M.
Hilton, Robert
Hamill, W. D. } equal.

PRACTICAL PHYSIOLOGY AND HISTOLOGY.

Graham, R. A. L.	Grills, G. H.
M'Master, A. B.	

MEDICINE.

M'Cay, David.	Simpson, Wm.

SURGERY.

Second Year.

M'Cutcheon, O. E., B.A. | Stewart, R. W. G.

First Year.

M'Dade, C. E., B.A. | M'Cay, David.
M'Master, A. B.

MATERIA MEDICA AND THERAPEUTICS.

Donnelly, Hugh.

MIDWIFERY, GYNÆCOLOGY, AND DISEASES OF CHILDREN.

Stewart R. W. G. | Fleck, David.
M'Cutcheon, O. E., B.A. | Hicks, G. A.

CHEMISTRY.

Senior Division.

Hilton, Robert.

Junior Division,

Hogg, W. J. | Beford, J. H., B.A.

PRACTICAL CHEMISTRY (ARTS AND MEDICINE).

Junior Division.

(Sproull, Eleanor R.] | Miskelly, S. S.
Smith, J. A. | Mathewson, Robert.

ZOOLOGY (ARTS AND MEDICINE).

Senior.

Hamill, W. D.

Junior.

Heron, A. G. | M'Mordie, David.
Rankin, J. O. | Black, A. L.

FACULTY OF LAW

COMMON AND CRIMINAL LAW.

— M'Cutcheon, R. R., B.A.

EQUITY AND BANKRUPTCY.

Irwin, Alexander, B.A.
[Magee, J. J., non-matriculated, } equal.

LAW OF PROPERTY.

Purvis, W. J., B.A | Robb, J. H.

CIVIL LAW.

Irvin, Alexander, B.A.   { [Wilson, Joseph, non-matriculated.]

JURISPRUDENCE.

Law Students.

Barkley, Matthew, B.A. | Robb, J. H.

Arts Students.

[Crawford, Florence.]

SUMMER PRIZEMEN, 1895.

BOTANY.

Senior.

Bles, W. A.

Junior.

Adams, John. | Hunter, W. M.
Rowan, M. L., B.A.

PRACTICAL CHEMISTRY.

[Tate, Isabel Adney.] } equal. | M'Master, A. B.
Beatty, W. R. | Grills, G. H.

MEDICAL JURISPRUDENCE.

Cousins, W. J.

SYSTEMATIC PATHOLOGY.

Fleck, David.

PRACTICAL PHARMACY.

Whyte, J. E.

B.—DEGREES, DIPLOMAS, HONOURS, &c., obtained by STUDENTS of the COLLEGE at the EXAMINATIONS of the ROYAL UNIVERSITY OF IRELAND IN 1895.

FACULTY OF ARTS.

Autumn, 1895.

Studentship.

IN MATHEMATICAL SCIENCE.

Leathem, John G.

Autumn, 1895.

M.A. DEGREE EXAMINATION.

HONOURS IN MENTAL SCIENCE.

First Class.

* Magill, Robert.

HONOURS IN MATHEMATICAL SCIENCE.

First Class.

Leathem, John G.

Pass.

Clements, Mary R.	Rodgers, William.
Johnson, William S.	

Summer, 1895.

B.A. DEGREE EXAMINATION.

Pass.

Breakey, William E.	Lewis, Samuel.
Carlisle, John M'C.	M'Conachie, John H.
Clements, Gordon T.C.	M'Crum, Joseph.
Cully, James.	Martin, Samuel H.
Hagan, James.	Oliver, John.
Heney, John.	Quinn, James.
Hogg, James A.	Rea, George W. D.
Johnston, Robert.	Stean, David M.
Johnston, Samuel K.	Wilson, Samuel.

Autumn, 1895.

B.A. DEGREE EXAMINATION.

EXHIBITIONS.

The names of those disqualified by University standing, age, or otherwise, are printed in *italics.*

First Class—£42 each.

M'Culla, James	Wallace, John S.

Second Class—£21 each.

Brown, John W.	*M'Bride, James A.*
Buchanan, Alex. C.	Megaw, John W. D.
Haire, James.	Purvis, William J.

HONOURS IN ANCIENT CLASSICS.

First Class.
M'Culla, James.

Second Class.
Buchanan, Alexander C.

HONOURS IN LOGIC, METAPHYSICS, ETHICS, AND HISTORY OF PHILOSOPHY,

Second Class.

Haire, James.	Simpson, Robert T.

* Awarded a Gold Medal and a Special Prize of £50 for highly distinguished answering.

HONOURS IN LOGIC, METAPHYSICS, HISTORY OF PHILOSOPHY, AND
POLITICAL ECONOMY.
Second Class.
Purvis, William J.

HONOURS IN CIVIL AND CONSTITUTIONAL HISTORY, POLITICAL ECONOMY,
AND GENERAL JURISPRUDENCE.
First Class.
Wallace, John S.

HONOURS IN MATHEMATICAL SCIENCE.
Second Class.

Miskelly, Samuel S. (Sch.).	Boas, Walter P.
Harvey, Francis W.	

HONOURS IN MATHEMATICAL AND EXPERIMENTAL PHYSICS.
Second Class.
M'Bride, James A.

HONOURS IN EXPERIMENTAL PHYSICS AND CHEMISTRY.
First Class.
Brown, John W.

HONOURS IN BIOLOGICAL SCIENCE.
Second Class.
Megaw, John W. D.
Pass.

Ahnern, Lilas J.	Johnston, James H. B.
Boyd, Andrew.	Kerr, Samuel P.
Dickson, Robert J.	Megaw, William.
Dodds, Joseph.	Rice, William A.

Summer, 1895.

SECOND UNIVERSITY EXAMINATION IN ARTS.
EXHIBITIONS AND HONOURS.
EXHIBITIONS.
First Class—£30 each.

Rice, James (sch.)	Leathem, William H.

Second Class—£18 each.

Beara, Thomas J.	Fullerton, Joseph A.
M'Neill, William.	

HONOURS IN LATIN.

First Class.

Leathem, William H.

Second Class.

White, William G.	Beare, Thomas J.
M'Neill, William.	Fullerton, Joseph A.

HONOURS IN GREEK.

Second Class.

Leathem, William H.

HONOURS IN ENGLISH.

First Class.

Leathem, William H.

Second Class.

Crawford, Florence.	Rice, James (Sch.)
M'Neill, William.	

HONOURS IN LOGIC.

First Class.

White, William G.	Beare, Thomas J.

Second Class.

Fullerton, Joseph A.	Leathem, William H.

HONOURS IN MATHEMATICS.

First Class.

Rice, James (Sch.)

HONOURS IN MATHEMATICAL PHYSICS.

First Class.

Rice, James (Sch.)

HONOURS IN EXPERIMENTAL PHYSICS.

Rice, James (Sch.)

Pass.

Barkley, William.	Dunn, Andrew.
Beare, Thomas J.	Fullerton, Joseph A.
Beatty, Martyn W.	Graham, Robert A. L.
Bradford, Charles C.	Hamill, William D.
Bright, James.	Harwood, Marion F.
Connolly, Alexander W.	Hilton, Robert.
Crawford, Florence.	Johnston, James.
Culbert, Thomas E.	Leathem, William H.
Dewar, David.	Lewis Wilfred J.

Pass—con.

M'Cardion, Robert.
M'Fetridge, William.
M'Kee, Frederick C.
M'Larnon, William K.
M'Mullan, William R.
M'Neill, William.
Moore, Arthur J. O. (Sch.)
Orr, William R.
Peek, Robert J. M.
Park, Samuel.

Rice, James (Sch.)
Smet, James R.
Todd, Ebenezer W.
Waddell, Hugh.
Warnock, Thomas A.
Whaley, John.
White, Frederick W.
White, William G.
Workman, Samuel.

Summer, 1895.

FIRST UNIVERSITY EXAMINATION IN ARTS.

EXHIBITIONS AND HONOURS.

EXHIBITIONS.

The names of those disqualified by age or otherwise are printed in *italics*

First Class, £30 each.

M'Cutcheon, Katharine S. H. (Sch.)
Paul, Francis J. (Sch.)
Harvey, Thomas R. (Sch.)

Porter, Samuel C. (Sch.)
Macafee, William.
Armstrong, Frederick W

Second Class, £15 each.

Minford, William.
Steepe, William A.

Hawthorne, John.

HONOURS IN LATIN.

First Class.

M'Cutcheon, Katharine S. H. (Sch.)
Armstrong, Frederick W.

Paul, Francis J. (Sch.)
Macafee, William.

Second Class

Porter, Samuel C. (Sch.)
Harvey, Thomas R. (Sch.)

Minford, William.

HONOURS IN GREEK.

First Class.

Armstrong, Frederick W.
Paul, Francis J. (Sch.)

M'Cutcheon, Katharine S. H. (Sch.)

Second Class.

Macafee, William.
Porter, Samuel C. (Sch.)

Minford, William.

HONOURS IN FRENCH.

Second Class.

Harvey, Thomas R. (Sch.)

HONOURS IN GERMAN.
First Class.
Hawthorne, John.

HONOURS IN ENGLISH.
First Class.

Paul, Francis J. (Sch.) | Harvey, Thomas E. (Sch.)

Second Class.
M'Cutcheon, Katherine S. H. (Sch.)
Porter, Samuel C. (Sch.)

HONOURS IN MATHEMATICS.
First Class.
Stoops, William A.

Second Class.
Harvey, Thomas E. (Sch.)
M'Cutcheon, Katherine S. H. (Sch.)

HONOURS IN NATURAL PHILOSOPHY.
First Class.
Paul, Francis J. (Sch.)
Second Class.

Stoops, William A.
MacGiffin, Henry A. | Harvey, Thomas E. (Sch.)

The following Candidates were also declared qualified to compete for Honours, but some of them did not present themselves for the Oral Examination.

ENGLISH.

Armstrong, Frederick W. | Macafee, William.

NATURAL PHILOSOPHY.
Porter, Samuel C. (Sch.)

Pass.

Armstrong, Frederick W.
Armstrong, Samuel G.
Carson, Thomas A.
Dobbin, William T.
Dunwoodie, John.
Ellison, Samuel C.
Finlay, Francis C.
Galway, John C.
Gamble, Joseph S

Hamilton, Samuel J.
Harvey, Thomas E. (Sch.).
Hawthorne, John.
Heron, Archibald O.
Jackson, Oswald E.
Johnston, John J. K.
Jones, George J.
Kelly, George.
Macafee, William.

Pass.—con.

M'Carroll, John C.
M'Cutcheon, Katherine S. H. (Sch.).
MacGiffin, Henry A.
M'Ilhatton, William.
M'Murray, John.
Minford, William.
Morrison, Samuel W.

Patterson, James M.
Paul, Francis J. (Sch.).
Peacock, Chrsmt.
Porter, Samuel C. (Sch.).
Smith, Hugh B.
Steen, John E.
Stoops, William A.
Williams, Robert A.

Autumn, 1895.

FIRST UNIVERSITY EXAMINATION IN ARTS.

Pass.

Baird, William.
Forgie, Alexander.

Latimer, William J.
Moore, Samuel B. W.

FACULTY OF LAW.

LL.B. DEGREE EXAMINATION.

Pass.

M'Ilwaine, Robert, M.A.　|　O'Kane, William M'K., B.A.

FIRST EXAMINATION IN LAW.

EXHIBITIONS.

Second Class, £10.
M'Cutcheon, Robert R., B.A.

HONOURS.

Second Class.

M'Cutcheon, Robert R., B.A.　|　Barkley, Matthew, B.A.

Pass.

Buchanan, James L.
Irwin, Alexander.

M'Cracken William J.
Whitaker, John M.

FACULTY OF MEDICINE.

Spring, 1895.

M.D. DEGREE EXAMINATION.
Morrow, John S., B.A.

Autumn, 1895.

M.D. DEGREE EXAMINATION.
Colville, James, B.A.

Autumn, 1895.

M.CH. DEGREE EXAMINATION.
Magrath, John, M.D.

Spring, 1895.

MEDICAL DEGREES EXAMINATION (M.B., B.CH., B.A.O.)

EXHIBITIONS.

First Class, £40.

Craig, James A.

Second Class, £20.

Houston, Thomas, B.A.

———

HONOURS

First Class.

Craig, James A.

Second Class.

Houston, Thomas, B.A.

Upper Pass Division.

Hanna, William, M.A.	Whitaker, Joseph H.
Trimble, Andrew.	

Pass Division.

Allen, Robert H.	Lowry, Joseph.
Boyd, Joseph D.	M'Burney, John H.
Herron, Walter.	M'Henry, James W.
Hunter, James, B.A.	Sommerville, David, B.A.
Johnston, Thomas J. W. A.	

———

Autumn, 1895.

MEDICAL DEGREES EXAMINATION (M.B. B.CH. B.A.O.).

Upper Pass Division.

Osborne, William A.

Pass Division.

Rhea, Charles.	M'William, William A.
Floyd, Samuel F.	Powell, Lilian A.
Irvine, Gilbert M., B.A.	Watson, Robert.

———

B.CH. DEGREE EXAMINATION.

Browne, James, M.D.

Spring, 1895.

THIRD EXAMINATION IN MEDICINE.

Pass Division.

Allen, Richard.	M'Cully, Andrew L.
Browne, Harry F.	Moran, Martin T.
Calwell, William.	Morrow, Ringland.
Canning, William.	Nevin, Robert.
Cowan, James.	Orr, Henry B.
Currell, Hugh.	Porter, William.
Flack, David.	Stuart, Robert G.
Lennon, John.	

———

Autumn, 1895.

THIRD EXAMINATION IN MEDICINE.

Upper Pass Division.

Hicks, George A.	Mewhirter, William H. W.
Jordan, William G.	Monypeny, Hiram J.
M'Cutcheon, Oliver E., B.A.	Stewart, James H.
M'Dade, Charles E., B.A.	

Pass Division.

Davis, John H.
Harvey, Joseph.
Johnston, John.
M'Comb, John H.
M'Kee, Frederick C.
M'Lorn, Robert R.

M'Murtry, John J. A. G.
Maguire, George J.
Robinson, Daniel S.
Stewart, Robert W. G.
Wilson, William J.

Spring, 1895.

SECOND EXAMINATION IN MEDICINE.

Upper Pass Division.

Grahame, Alexander.

Smiley, George K.

Pass Division.

Armstrong, William L.
Craig, Henry L.
Hanna, Henry, B.A.
Harbinson, George O. R.
Hill, Samuel.
Hogg, George A.

Irvine, Francis S.
Jones, William E. J.
Ross, Thomas S.
Scott, John.
Shaw, Robert A.
Whyte, James E.

Autumn, 1895.

SECOND EXAMINATION IN MEDICINE.

Upper Pass Division.

Brown, David.
Graham, Robert A. L.

Jefferson, George.
M'Master, Arthur R.

Pass Division.

Beatty, William R.
Brannan, John.
Crawford, Arthur W.
Henry, George H., B.A.

Kennedy, Thomas.
Kerr, Robert.
Martin, Joseph.
Moran, Patrick J.

Summer, 1895.

FIRST EXAMINATION IN MEDICINE.

HONOURS IN CHEMISTRY.

Second Class.

Hamill, William D.

HONOURS IN EXPERIMENTAL PHYSICS.

Second Class.

Hamill, William D.

Pass.

Clements, John E.
Crawford, Annie H.
Hamill, William D.
Hunter, William M.
Huston, Alexandrina C.
Kennedy, Alexander F.
Luke, George P.

Martin, Edward W. S.
Park, Samuel.
Thomson, Alfred M.
Tierney, John.
Waddell, James.
West, John W.

Appendix to Report of the President

Autumn, 1895.

FIRST EXAMINATION IN MEDICINE.

HONOURS IN EXPERIMENTAL PHYSICS.

Second Class.

Simpson, John E.

Pass.

Barkley, William.	Robb, James J.
Crooks, Emily M.	Rowan, Marriott L., B.A.
Huston, Thomas.	Simpson, John E.
M'Garrison, Robert.	Watson, William.

Summer, 1896.

SCHOOL OF ENGINEERING.

B.E. DEGREE EXAMINATION.

EXHIBITION.

First Class—£42.

Sides, John F.

HONOURS.

First Class.

Sides, John F.

SECOND PROFESSIONAL EXAMINATION IN ENGINEERING.

EXHIBITION.

First Class, £36.

Galley, Thomas A.

HONOURS.

First Class.

Galley, Thomas A.

Second Class.

Orr, William R.

Pass.

Bright, James.

TABLE VIII.—STUDENTS OF THE COLLEGE WHO HAVE GAINED JUNIOR FELLOWSHIPS, STUDENTSHIPS, SCHOLARSHIPS, EXHIBITIONS, OR PRIZES IN THE ROYAL UNIVERSITY OF IRELAND, SINCE ITS ESTABLISHMENT.

The names of those who were disqualified by University standing, or age, are printed in *Italics.*

JUNIOR FELLOWSHIPS.

Morton, William B., M.A., in Mathematics, 1894.
Woodburn, George, M.A., in Mental and Moral Science, 1894.

UNIVERSITY STUDENTSHIPS.

Tate, James, in Mathematics, 1883, £100 for five years.
M'Quitty, W. B., in Experimental Science, 1894, £100 for five years.
FitzHenry, W. A., in Mental and Moral Science, 1885, £100 for five years.
Boyd, Andrew, in Civil and Constitutional History, Jurisprudence, and Political Philosophy, 1886, £100 for five years.
Orr, W. McFadden, in Mathematics, 1887, £100 for five years.
Rowan, W. H., in Classics, 1889, £100 for three years.
Woodburn, George, in Mental and Moral Science, 1890, £100 for three years.
Montgomery, Robert, in Classics, 1891, £100 for three years.
Haslett, Thomas, in Mental and Moral Science, 1891, £100 for three years.
Morton, W. B., in Mathematical Science, 1892, £100 for three years.
Moore, Benjamin, in Experimental Science, 1899, £100 for three years.
M'Elderry, Robert K., in Classics, 1893, £100 for three years.
Cochrane, John, in History and Political Science, 1893, £100 for three years.
Dornan, Frederick G., in Experimental Science, 1894, £100 for three years.
Latham, John G., in Mathematical Science, 1895, £100 for three years.

UNIVERSITY SCHOLARSHIPS.

Orr, W. M'F., in Mathematics, 1883, £50 for three years.
Johnson, W. S., in Classics, 1884, £50 for three years.
Alexander, J. J., in Mathematics, 1884, £50 for three years.
Everett, Alice, in Mathematics, 1885, £50 for three years.
Porter, W. H., in Classics, 1886, £50 for three years.
Haslett, W. W., in Classics, 1886, £50 for three years.
Williamson, W. H., in Mathematics, 1886, £50 for three years.
Major, H. W., in Mathematics, 1886, £50 for three years.

DR. HENRY HUTCHINSON STEWART SCHOLARSHIP.

Wilson, Mary, in Arts, 1886.
Baxter, J. S., in Arts, 1890.
Woods, W. J., in Medicine, 1890.
Chapman, Agnes H., in Arts, 1892.

AT M.A. EXAMINATION.

Louden, James, a Gold Medal, 1884.
Boyd, Andrew, a Special Prize, 1885, £20.
FitzHenry, W. A., a Gold Medal, 1885.
M'Quitty, W. B., a Special Prize, 1885, £90.
Hunter, James, a Special Prize, 1885, £50.
Orr, W. McF., a Gold Medal, 1887.
Campbell, J. R., a Special Prize, 1887, £50.
Woodburn, George, a Gold Medal, 1889.
Witherow, J. M., a Special Prize, 1891, £50.
Haslett, W. W., Special Prize, 1892, £50.
Heron, Richard O., Special Prize, 1893, £40.

At B.A. Examination.

Harrison, Thomas, First Class Exhibition, 1882,				—
Johnston, John,	"	"	"	£50.
Jones, R. M.,	"	"	"	£50.
M'Vicker, J. W.,	"	"	"	£50.
Campbell, J. E.,	"	"	1883.	£50.
Darbishire, H. D.,	"	"	"	£50.
Hunter, James,	"	"	"	£50.
Louden, James, First Class Exhibition,			"	£30.
Campbell, John, Second Class		"	"	£25.
Chambers, Joseph,	"	"	"	—
Boyd, Andrew, First Class		"	1884,	£50.
Boyd, R. W.,	"	"	"	—
FitzHenry, W. A.,	"		"	£50.
M'Quitty, W. B.,	"	"	"	£50.
Glass, Thomas, Second Class		"	"	—
Henderson, Robert,	"	"	"	£25.
Hillen, W. M.,	"	"	"	£25.
M'Anlis, Thomas,	"	"	"	£25.
Russell, W. A.,	"	"	"	£25.
Cunning, David, First Class		"	1885,	—
Orr, W. M'F.,	"	"	"	£50.
Orr, W. M'F., Special Prize,		"	"	£50.
Rea, J. C., First Class Exhibition,			"	—
Russell, William,	"	"	"	£50.
Stewart, Thomas,	"	"	"	£50.
Vance, John,	"	"	"	£50.
Cromie, R. S., Second Class		"	"	£25.
Dill, A. H.,	"	"	"	—
Donald, R. J. F.,	"	"	"	—
Fitzsimons, J. H.,	"	"	"	£25.
M'Neill, Robert,	"	"	"	£25.
Priestley, James,	"	"	"	£25.
Alexander, J. J., First Class		"	1886,	£50.
Dunn, William,	"	"	"	£50.
Johnson, W. S.,	"	"	"	£50.
Wheeler, G. H.,	"	"	"	£50.
Jamison, Daniel, Second Class		"	"	£25.
Montgomery, Robert,	"	"	"	—
Bowan, W. H., First Class		"	1887,	£50.
Brown, R. K., Second Class		"	"	—
Browne, J. A.,	"	"	"	£25.
Campbell, Robert,	"	"	"	£25.
Henderson, William,	"	"	"	£25.
Keightley, F. R.,	"	"	"	—
McConnell, James,	"	"	"	—
Salters, James,	"	"	"	—
Wilson, Mary,	"	"	"	£25.
Allison, W. M. B., First Class		"	1888,	£50.
Haslett, W. W.,	"	"	"	£50.
Stewart, J. A.,	"	"	"	£50.
Woodburn, George,	"	"	"	£50.
Adams, J. J., Second Class		"	"	£25.
Jackson, Maud S.,	"	"	"	—
Montgomery, Robert,	"	"	"	£25.
Semple, John,	"	"	"	—
Williamson, W. H.,	"	"	"	£25.
Archer, J. H., First Class		"	1889,	£42.
Extracon, Sara,	"	"	"	—
Haslett, Thomas,	"	"	"	£42.
Kirk, T. S.,	"	"	"	£42.
Morton, W. S.,	"	"	"	£42.
Witherow, J. M.,	"	"	"	£42.

At B.A. Examination—con.

Wood, Jackson, First Class Exhibition,	1889	—
Cotter, W. E. P., Second Class	,,	,,	£21.
Leathem, R. R. L.,	,,	,,	£91.
Hanna, William, First Class	,,	1890,	£49.
Heron, R. C.,	,,	,,	£42.
Cochrane, John, Second Class	,,	,,	£21.
Lee, James,	,,	,,	£21.
M'Kee, R. H., Second Class	,,	,,	—
Moore, Benjamin,	,,	,,	£21.
Walker, James,	,,	,,	£21.
Wylie, John,	,,	,,	—
Leathem, John G., First Class	,,	1891,	£42.
M'Elderry, R. K.,	,,	,,	£42.
Baxter, J. G., Second Class	,,	,,	£2.
Bradshaw, J. M.,	,,	,,	£91.
Hers, James, B. e.s.,	,,	,,	—
Ashmore, . H., First Class	,,	1892,	£42.
Donnan, F. G.,	,,	,,	£42.
Houston, W. A.,	,,	,,	£42.
Gillespie, J. T., Second Class	,,	,,	£91.
Maxell, D. E.,	,,	,,	£21.
O'Neill, F. W. S.,	,,	,,	£91.
Chapman, Agnes R., First Class	,,	1893,	£42.
Gillespie, John H.,	,,	,,	£42.
Hanna, Henry,	,,	,,	£42.
Henry, Robert M.,	,,	,,	£42.
Rodgers, William,	,,	,,	£42.
Johnstone, Robt. J., Second Class	,,	,,	£21.
Martin, Thomas,	,,	,,	£21.
Sayers, William J.	,,	,,	£21.
Lodin, George T., First Class	,,	1894,	£42.
M'Mullan, John J.,	,,	,,	£42
Magill, Robert,	,,	,,	£42.
Buchanan, Jas. L., Second Class	,,	,,	£21.
Mistally, William,	,,	,,	£2L
M'Calla, James, First Class,	,,	1895,	£42.
Wallace, John S.	,,	,,	£42.
Brown, John W., Second Class,	,,	,,	£21.
Buchanan, Alexander C.,	,,	,,	£2L
Haire, James,	,,	,,	£21.
M'Bride, James A.	,,	,,	—
Magaw, John W. D.	,,	,,	£91.
Purvis, William J.	,,	,,	£21.

At Second Arts Examination.

Russell, W. A., First Class Exhibition,	1892,	£40.
Derbishire, H. D., Second Class	,,	,,	£90.
Hunter, James	,,	,,	£90.
Campbell, J. E.,	,,	,,	£20.
Lennax, M. E. M., First Class	,,	1893,	£40.
Donald, R. J. F., Second Class	,,	,,	£90.
Rae, J. C.	,,	,,	—
Orr, W. M'F., First Class	,,	1894,	£40.
M'Neill, Robert,	,,	,,	£40.
Crosbie, R. S., Second Class	,,	,,	£90.
Anderson, Alice M.,	,,	,,	£20.
Haslett, Annie W.,	,,	,,	£90.
Priestley, James,	,,	,,	£40.
Johnann, W. S., First Class	,,	1895,	£40.
Wheeler, G. H., Second Class	,,	,,	£90.
Brown, G. W.,	,,	,,	£20.
Macdonnell, A. J. P.,	,,	,,	£90.

AT SECOND ARTS EXAMINATION—*con.*

Name	Class	Year	Amount
Irwin, William,	First Class Exhibition,	1885,	£20.
Dick, J. S.,	" "	"	£20.
Bowan, W. H.,	" "	1886,	£40.
Luke, E. H.,	" "	"	£40.
Montgomery, Robert,	" "	"	£40.
Stern, D. M.	" "	"	£40.
Semple, John,	Second Class	"	—
Campbell, Robert,	" "	"	£20.
Everat, Alice,	" "	"	£20.
Padlow, T. B.,	" "	"	£20.
Wyfie, John,	" "	"	£20.
Jamison, Alexander,	" "	"	£20.
Haslett, W. W.,	First Class	1887,	£40.
Stewart, J. A.,	" "	"	£40.
Colter, W. E. P., Second Class	"	"	£20.
Williamson, W. H.,	" "	"	£20.
Hamill, James,	" "	"	£20.
Morton, W. B.,	First Class	1888,	£40.
Archer, J. H.,	" "	"	£40.
Lea, James,	" "	"	£40.
Megaw, R. D.,	Second Class,	"	£20.
Dickie, A. A.,	" "	"	£20.
Estricen, Sara,	" "	"	—
Bradshaw, J. M., First Class	"	1889,	£30.
Moore, Benjamin, Second Class	"	"	£18.
Walker, James,	" "	"	£18.
M'Cracken, W. J.,	" "	"	£18.
Haron, R. C.,	" "	"	£18.
Donald, A. L.,	" "	"	£18.
Hoemion, Thomas,	" "	"	£18.
Lauthem, J. G., First Class	"	1890,	£36.
Gillespie, J. T.,	" "	"	£36
M'Elderry, W. K.,	" "	"	£36.
Baxter, J. S.,	" "	"	£36.
Toye, Thomas, Second Class	"	"	£18.
Gillespie, Samuel,	" "	"	£18.
Megaw, David,	" "	"	£18.
Fullerton, W. A.,	" "	"	£18.
Wilson, W. A.,	" "	"	£18.
Donnan, F. G., First Class	"	1891,	£30.
Ashmore, B. H.,	" "	"	£30.
Hoaxton, W. A.,	" "	"	£30.
M'Hitrick, Alex., Second Class	"	"	£18.
Porter, John A.,	" "	"	£18.
Bowan, M. L.,	" "	"	£18.
Gillespie, J. R., First Class	"	1892,	£36.
Rodgers, William,	" "	"	£36.
Crawford, W. M.,	" "	"	£36.
M'Cutcheon, R. E., Second Class	"	"	£18.
Reid, D. D.,	" "	"	£18.
Pyper, John,	" "	"	£18.
Henry, R. M.,	" "	"	£18.
Locke, George T., First Class	"	1893,	£36.
Ross, Walter P.,	" "	"	£36.
Miskelly, William,	" "	"	£36.
Buchanan, James L., Second Class	"	"	£18.
Minford, John Y.,	" "	"	£18.
M'Calla, James, First Class	"	1894,	£36.
Miskelly, Samuel S.,	" "	"	£36.
Buchanan, Alexander G.,	" "	"	£36.
Purvis, William J., Second Class	"	"	£18.
Sice, James, First Class	"	1895,	£36.

At Second Arts Examination—con.

Leathem, William H , First Class Exhibition, 1896, £36.
Beare, Thomas J., Second Class   „   „   £18.
M'Neill, William,   „   „   „   £18
Fullerton, Joseph A.   „   „   „   £18.

At First University Examination.

Gorman, W. T., Second Class Exhibition, 1892, £18.
Keane, A. T.,   „   „   £15.
M'Neill, Robert, First Class   „   1893, £30.
Orr, W. M'F.,   „   „   £30.
Cromie, E. F., Second Class   „   „   £15.
Anderson, Alice M.,   „   „   £15.
Brown, G. W., First Class   „   1894, £30.
Wheeler, G. H., Second Class   „   „   £15.
Morton, Hamilton,   „   „   £15.
Alexander, J. J.,   „   „   £13.
Irwin, William,   „   „   £15.
Dick, J. S.,   „   „   £15.
Semple, John, First Class   „   1895, —
Everett, Alice, First Class   „   „   £30.
Montgomery, Robert,   „   „   £20.
Bowen, W. H.,   „   „   £30.
Luke, F. H.,   „   „   £20.
Campbell, Robert, Second Class   „   „   £15.
Pedlow, T. B.,   „   „   £15.
Hamill, James,   „   „   £15.
Jamison, Alexander,   „   „   £15.
Haslett, W. W.,   First Class   „   1896, £30.
Williamson, W. H.,   „   „   £30
Cotter, W. E. P., Second Class   „   „   £15
Allison, W. M. B.,   „   „   £15.
Stewart, J. A.,   „   „   £15.
Morton, W. B., First Class   „   1897, £30.
Archer, J. H.,   „   „   £30.
Lee, James,   „   „   £30.
Dickie, A. A., Second Class   „   „   £15.
Megaw, R. D.,   „   „   £13.
Donald, A. L.,   „   „   £15.
Heron, R. C.,   First Class   „   1898, £30.
Bradshaw, J. M.,   „   „   £30.
Woods, W. J.,   Second Class   „   „   £15.
Cochrane, John,   „   „   £15.
M'Cracken, W. J.,   „   „   £15.
Leathem, J. G.,   First Class   „   1899, £30.
Gillespie, J. T.,   „   „   £30.
M'Eldarry, R. K.,   „   „   £30.
Fullerton, W. A.,   „   „   £30.
Baxter, J. S.,   „   „   £30.
Megaw, David,   Second Class   „   „   £15.
Marjoribanks, N. B.,   „   „   £15.
Gillespie, Samuel,   „   „   £15.
Donnan, F. G.,   First Class   „   1890, £30.
Houston, W. A.,   „   „   £30.
Ashmore, B. H.,   „   „   £30.
M'Kitrick, Alexander,   „   „   £30.
Porter, J. A., Second Class   „   „   £18.
M'Cutcheon, O. E.,   „   „   £18.
M'Mullan, Frederick,   „   „   £18.
Bingham, B. W.,   „   „   £18.
Mercier, D. P.,   „   „   £18.
Rowan, M. L.,   „   „   £18.

At First University Examination—*con.*

Gillespie, J. R., First Class Exhibition, 1891,				£30.
Pyper, John,	„	„	„	£30.
Woodburn, J. B.,	„	„	„	£30
M'Cutcheon, R. H., Second Class	„	„	£15
Johnstone, R. J.,	„	„	„	£15.
Clements, Mary E.,	„	„	„	£15
Boas, W. P., First Class	„	1892,	£30.
Locke, G. T.,	„	„	„	£30.
Harvey, F. W.,	„	„	„	£30.
Adams, John,	„	„	„	£30.
M'Culla, James,	„	„	„	£30.
Miskelly, William,	„	„	„	£30.
Buchanan, J. L., Second Class	„	„	£15.
Minford, J. G.,	„	„	„	£15.
Clements, W. T.,	„	„	„	£15.
Miskelly, Samuel S., First Class	„	1893,	£30.
Purvis, William J., Second Class	„	„	£15.
Buchanan, Alexander C.,	„	„	„	£15.
Megaw, John W. D.,	„	„	„	£15.
Atkinson, George C.,	„	„	„	£15.
Brown, John W.,	„	„	„	£15.
Rice, James, First Class	„	1894,	£30.
Fullerton, Joseph A., Second Class	„	„	£15.
Lambson, William E.,	„	„	„	£15.
M'Neill, William,	„	„	„	£15.
Todd, Ebenezer W.,	„	„	„	£15.
Scott, James B.,	„	„	„	£15.
Hilton, Robert,	„	„	„	£15.
M'Cutcheon, Katherine S. H., First Class	„	1895,	£30.
Paul, Francis J.,	„	„	„	£30.
Harvey, Thomas E.,	„	„	„	£30.
Porter, Samuel C,	„	„	„	£30.
Macafee, William,	„	„	„	£30.
Armstrong, Frederick W.	„	„	„	£30.
Minford, William, Second Class	„	1895,	£15.
Stoops, William A.,	„	„	„	
Hawthorne, John	„	„	„	£15.

At LL.B. Examination.

Strahan, J. A.,	A Prize, 1882,	£50.
Corr, W. H.,	„	„	£25.
Waltz, W. N.,	„	1883,	£25.
Hamilton, A. B.,	„	1884,	£50.
Nelson, T. E.,	„	„	£25.
Harrison, Thomas,	„	1886,	£50.
Forbes, John,	„	„	£25.
Turnbull, M. H.,	„	1888,	£25.
Gibson, T. R.,	„	1889,	£21.
Johnston, Wm. J. A.,	„	1891,	£21.
Megaw, R. D., First Class Prize, 1892,	£42.
M'Cormick, J. W., Second Class Prize,	„	£21.
Archer, James H., Second Class Exhibition, 1893,	£21.

First Examination in Law.

Megaw, R. D., M.A.,   A Prize, 1891, £20.
Morell, David E., B.Mus., First Class Exhibition, 1894, £20.
M'Cutcheon, Robert B., Second Class   „   1895, £10.

At Medical Degrees Examination.

Haslett, R. W., Second Class Exhibition, 1882.
Campbell, Robert, Second Class Exhibition, £25.

At M.B. Examination.

White, William, Second Class Exhibition, 1884, —
Grainger, Thomas, ,, ,, £2A.
Redfern, J. J., First Class, ,, 1885, £50.
Thomson, G. S., Second Class ,, 1886, £25.
Mackinnch, H. L., ,, ,, 1887, £25.
Fullerton, Andrew, First Class ,, 1890, £40.
Woods, Wm. J., Second Class ,, 1893, £25.
Thompson, Wm. D. T., ,, ,, 1894, £25.
Watt, Robert, ,, ,, ,, £12.
Craig, James A., First Class ,, 1895, £40.
Houston, Thomas, Second Class ,, ,, £25.

At M.Ch. Examination.

Cowden, W. J., m.d., Special Prize, 1885, £90.

At M.A.O. Examination.

Redfern, J. J., Special Prize, 1885, £90.

At Third Examination in Medicine.

Hall, J. M., First Class Exhibition, 1888, —
Griffith, P. G., Second Class ,, 1889, —
Fullerton, Andrew, ,, ,, £90.
Woods, W. J., First Class ,, 1891, £30.
Jamison, Alexander, m.a., Second Class Exhibition,
1891, £20.
Leathem, B. R. L., b.a., ,, ,,
1891, £90.
M'Keown, R. J., Second Class Exhibition, 1892, £20.
Watt, Robert, ,, ,, £20.
Craig, James A., First Class ,, 1893, £30.

At Second Examination in Medicine.

Chambers, James, First Class Exhibition, 1882, —
Grainger, Thomas, Second Class ,, ,, £20.
M'Quitty, W. B., First Class ,, 1883, £40.
Buchanan, Andrew, Second Class ,, ,, £20.
Woods, E. M'N., ,, ,, 1884, £10.
Weatherup, William, ,, ,, 1885, £20.
Hall, J. M., First Class ,, 1886, —
Fullerton, Andrew, Second Class ,, 1888, £15.
Robertson, W. B., ,, ,, 1890, £15.
Jamison, Alex, m.a., ,, ,, ,, £15.
Woods, W. J., First Class ,, ,, £25.
Craig, J. A., Second Class ,, 1891, £15.
MacKeown, Wm. J., First Class ,, 1892, £25.
Beggs, Samuel T., Second Class ,, ,, £15.

At First Examination in Medicine.

Haslett, R. W., First Class Exhibition, 1884, £30.
Smiley, D. C., Second Class ,, ,, £15.
Morton, Hamilton, First Class ,, 1885, £30.
Wilson, Robert, Second Class ,, ,, £15.
Robertson, W. B., First Class ,, 1886, £30.
Moore, Benjamin, ,, ,, 1890, —
Houston Thomas, ,, ,, 1891, —
Osborne, W. A., ,, ,, 1892, £30.
Johnstone, B. J., Second Class ,, ,, £10.
Hanna, Henry, First Class ,, 1893, £20.
Scott, John, Second Class ,, ,, £10.

At B.E. Examination.

Burden, A. M., First Class Exhibition,   1885, £50.
Heron, James,   A Prize,   "   £20.
Graham, John, Second Class Exhibition,   1887, £25.
Phillips, J. St. J.,   "   "   1890, £21.
Sides, John F., First Class   "   1898, £12.

At Second Examination in Engineering.

Tate, C. L., First Class Exhibition,	1884,	£20	Prize.
Burden, A. M.,	"	"	£40.
Heron, James, Second Class	"	"	£30.
Anderson, J. T. N.,	"	1885,	£20.
Graham, John.	"	1886,	£20.
Greer, R. T.	"	"	1891,	£18.
Sides, John F., First Class	"	1894,	£35.
Gailey, Thomas A.,	"	1895,	£36.

At First Examination in Engineering.

Burden, A. M., First Class Exhibition,	1883,	£30.
Heron, James, Second Class	"	"	£15.
Anderson, J. T. N.,	"	1884,	£15.
Graham, John,	"	"	1884,	£15.
Moore, Benjamin,	"	"	1888,	£15.
Megaw, David,	"	"	1892,	—
Sides, John F.,	"	1893,	£18.
Gailey, Thomas A., First Class,	"	1894,	£30.

At Matriculation Examination.

Barnett, R. W., Second Class Exhibition, 1881, £12.
Gorman, W. T.,   "   "   £12.
Johnston, William,   "   "   "   £12.
Johnson, W. S., First Class   "   1883, £24.
Rowan, W. H.,   "   "   1884, £24.
Everett, Alice,   "   "   "   £24.

TABLE IX.—List of Sundry Students of the COLLEGE who have since 1st January, 1881, obtained distinctions in Universities other than the Royal University of IRELAND.

The date immediately following each name is that of the last Session in which the name of the Student appeared on the Roll of the College.

EGGLES, JOHN, M.A. (1876-77).
    1881. Wranglership, 14th place in the Mathematical Tripos, University of Cambridge.

NEWSOMB, J. C., M.A. (1876-77).
    1884. Scholarship (Classical), Trinity College, Dublin.
    1887. Classical Studentship, Trinity College, Dublin.

CHARLES, R. H., M.A. (1877-78).
    1881. Senior Moderatorship in Classics, and Junior Moderatorship in Ethics and Logics, University of Dublin.

CORRY, T. H., M.A. (1877-78).
    1881. Scholarship, Gonville and Caius College, Cambridge.

JOHNSTON, W. J., M.A. (1877–78).
  1883. Senior Moderatorship in Mathematics and Physics, University of Dublin.

WRIGHT, A. E., B.A. (1877–78).
  1882. Senior Moderatorship in Modern Literature, University of Dublin.

KNOWLES, T. T., M.A. (1878–79).
  1882. Wranglership, 19th place in Mathematical Tripos, University of Cambridge.

SEAVER, RICHARD W., M.A. (1879–80).
  1881. Scholarship (Classical), University of Dublin.
  1883. Senior Moderatorship in Ethics and Logics, and Junior Moderatorship in Classics, University of Dublin.

REID, J. S., B.A. (1880–81).
  1882. Foundation Scholarship, Lincoln College, Oxford.

M'FARLAND, R. A. H., M.A. (1880–81).
  1882. Scholarship, Gonville and Caius College, Cambridge.
  1883. Wranglership, 6th place in Mathematical Tripos, University of Cambridge.
  „   Exhibition, Gonville and Caius College, Cambridge.

SEMPLE, R. H., M.A. (1880–81).
  1881. Sizarship, St. John's College, Cambridge.
  „   Exhibition, Goldsmiths' Company, University of Cambridge.
  „   Exhibition at First B.A. Examination in Mathematics, University of London.

ANDERSON, W. C. F., M.A. (1881–82).
  1882. Foundation Scholarship, University of Durham.
  „   Newby Scholarship, University of Durham.
  1883. First Year Scholarship, University of Durham.
  „   University Classical Scholarship, University of Durham.
  1884. Calbet Prize for Essay on Moral Philosophy, University of Durham.
  „   Adam de Browne Exhibition, Oriel College, Oxford.
  1885. Second Class in Classical Moderations, University of Oxford.
  1887. Second Class in Final Classical School, University of Oxford.

LARMOR, ALEXANDER, M.A. (1881–82).
  1881. First Entrance Scholarship in Mathematics, Clare College, Cambridge.
  1883. Foundation Scholarship, Clare College, Cambridge.
  1884. Wranglership, 11th place in Mathematical Tripos, University of Cambridge:
  1886. Berkeley Fellowship, Owen's College, Manchester.
  „   Fellowship, Clare College, Cambridge.

CAMPBELL, ALBERT (1882–83).
  1884. Foundation Scholarship, Corpus Christi College, Cambridge.
  1885. First Senior Optime, University of Cambridge.

M'VICKER, J. W., B.A. (1882–83).
  1883. Scholarship in Mathematics, Worcester College, Oxford.

STEWART, D. A., M.A. (1882–83).
  1881. First Mathematical Scholarship, Caius College, Cambridge.
  1883. Foundation Scholarship, Caius College, Cambridge.
  „   Mathematical Scholarship, University of London.
  „   Goldsmith Exhibition, University of Cambridge.

RUSSELL, W. A., B.A. (1883–84).
  1883. Exhibition, St. John's College, Cambridge.
    „   Sizarship, St. John's College, Cambridge.
  1885. Goldsmith Exhibition, University of Cambridge.
  1886. Honours in Classical Tripos, University of Cambridge.

CAMPBELL, J. E., M.A. (1883–84).
  1883. Mathematical Scholarship, Hertford College, Oxford.
  1885. Junior University Mathematical Scholarship, and First Class in Mathematical Moderations, University of Oxford.
  1887. First Class in Final Mathematical School, University of Oxford.
  1887. Fellowship, Hertford College, Oxford.
  1888. Senior Mathematical Scholarship, University of Oxford.

DARBISHIRE, H. D., B.A. (1883–84).
  1883. Sizarship, St. John's College, Cambridge.
  1885. Honours in Classical Tripos, University of Cambridge.
  1888. Foundation Scholarship, St. John's College, Cambridge.
  1889. M'Mahon Law Scholarship, St. John's College, Cambridge.
  1892. Fellowship, St. John's College, Cambridge.

BARNETT, R. W. (1881–82).
  1885. Third Class in Classical Moderations, University of Oxford.
  1887. Second Class in Jurisprudence, University of Oxford.

ORR, W. M'F., M.A. (1884–85).
  1884. Foundation Scholarship, St. John's College, Cambridge.
  1886. Exhibition in St. John's College, Cambridge.
  1888. Senior Wrangler in Mathematical Tripos, University of Cambridge.
  1889. First Class in Mathematical Tripos, Part II.

TATE, JAMES, B.A. (1883–84).
  1885. Sixteenth Wrangler, University of Cambridge.
  1886. Foundation Scholarship, St. John's College, Cambridge.

STEEDE, E. B. (1885–86).
  1886. Science Scholarship, Trinity College, Dublin.
  1887. Mathematical Studentship, Trinity College, Dublin.
  1889. Bishop Law Mathematical Premium, Trinity College, Dublin.

PORTER, W. H. (1885–86).
  1887. Scholarship, Lincoln College, Oxford.
  1888. Goldsmith Exhibition, University of Oxford.
  1889. Second Class in Classical Moderations, University of Oxford.
  1893. Chancellor's Prize for English Prose Essay, University of Oxford.

GREGG, JAMES (1880–81).
  1886. First Science Scholarship, Trinity College, Dublin.

LUNN, E. H., B.A. (1886–87).
  1886. Classical Scholarship, Trinity College, Dublin.

MAJOR, H. W. (1887–88).
  1888. First Entrance Scholarship in Mathematics, Queen's College, Cambridge.
  1889. Foundation Scholarship in Mathematics, Queen's College, Cambridge.
  1891. Second Class Honours in Mathematical Tripos, University of Cambridge.

M'BRIDE, E. W. (1887–88).
  1888. Entrance Exhibition, St. John's College, Cambridge.
  1889. Exhibition in Natural Science, St. John's College, Cambridge.
  1890. B.Sc. with First Class Honours and Exhibition in Natural Science, University of London.
    ,, First Class Honours at Natural Science Tripos, Part I., University of Cambridge.
    ,, Foundation Scholarship, St. John's College, Cambridge.
  1891. First Class Honours in Natural Science Tripos, Part II. University of Cambridge.
    ,, Hughes Prize, St. John's College, Cambridge.
  1892. Appointed Demonstrator in Natural Science at University of Cambridge.
  1893. Elected Fellow of St. John's College, Cambridge.
    ,, The Walsingham Medal for original work in Natural Science, University of Cambridge.

HASLETT, W. W., M.A. (1888–89).
  1888. Entrance Exhibition, St. John's College, Cambridge.
  1890. Foundation Scholarship, St. John's College, Cambridge.
  1891. First Class Honours in Classical Tripos, Part I., University of Cambridge.
  1892. First Class Honours in Classical Tripos, Part II., University of Cambridge.

MONTGOMERY, ROBERT, B.A. (1887–88).
  1889. Foundation Sizarship, and First Class Honours in Classics, Trinity College, Cambridge.
  1890. Foundation Scholarship, Trinity College, Cambridge.
  1891. First Class Honours in Classical Tripos, University of Cambridge.

ALEXANDER, J. J., M.A. (1887–88).
  1887. Entrance Exhibition, St. John's College, Cambridge.
  1889. Foundation Scholarship, St. John's College, Cambridge.
  1890. Wranglership, Seventh place in Mathematical Tripos, University of Cambridge.

LEE, JAMES (1888–89).
  1889. Entrance Exhibition, St. John's College, Cambridge.

MORTON, W. B., M.A. (1888–89).
  1889. Entrance Exhibition, St. John's College, Cambridge.
  1891. Foundation Scholarship, St. John's College, Cambridge.
  1892. Wranglership, Eighth place in Mathematical Tripos, University of Cambridge.

COTTER, W. E. P., B.A. (1888–89).
  1889. Classical Scholarship, Trinity College, Dublin.

HENRY, R. C. (1889–90).
  1889. Exhibition, St. John's College, Cambridge.
  1891. Foundation Sizarship, St. John's College, Cambridge.
  1893. Wranglership, Twentieth place in Mathematical Tripos University of Cambridge

STEWART, J. A., B.A. (1888–89).
  1889. Exhibition, St. John's College, Cambridge.
  1891. Foundation Scholarship, St. John's College, Cambridge.

D

KEIGHTLEY, F. R., B.A. (1886–7).
1890. Third Class Honours in Historical Tripos, University of Cambridge.

LAATHEM, J. G. (1890–91).
1891. Entrance Exhibition, St. John's College, Cambridge.
1894. Hughes Prize, St. John's College, Cambridge.
„   Wranglership, Fourth place in Mathematical Tripos, University of Cambridge.
1896. First Division of First Class in Mathematical Tripos, Part II., University of Cambridge.
„   Sir Isaac Newton Studentship, University of Cambridge.

M'ELDERRY, R. K. (1890–91).
1891. Entrance Exhibition, St. John's College, Cambridge.
1893. Hughes Prize, St. John's College, Cambridge.
1894. First Class, 2nd Division, in Classical Tripos, Part I., University of Cambridge.
1895. First Class in Classical Tripos, Part II., University of Cambridge, with Star for distinguished answering in History Section.

M'VICKER, C. E. (1890–91).
1892. Wranglership, Seventeenth place in Mathematical Tripos, University of Cambridge.

BOAS, W. P. (1891–93).
1892. Entrance Exhibition, St. John's College, Cambridge.
1894. Exhibition, St. John's College, Cambridge.

HOUSTON, W. A. (1891–92).
1892. Entrance Exhibition, St. John's College, Cambridge.
1894. Foundation Scholarship, St. John's College, Cambridge.
1896. Wranglership, Fifth place in Mathematical Tripos, University of Cambridge.

LOCKE, O. T. (1893–94).
1894. Entrance Exhibition, St. John's College, Cambridge.
„   Foundation Scholarship, St. John's College, Cambridge.

ROSS, A. A. (1893–94).
1894. Entrance Exhibition, St. John's College, Cambridge.

CLEMENTS, W. T. (1893–94).
1894. Entrance Exhibition, St. John's College, Cambridge.

BAXTER, J. SINCLAIR (1893–94).
1894. LL.B. with First Class Honours, London University.

MENAW, R. D.
1894. Prize of £50 for distinguished answering at the Examination for the Reid Professorship, Trinity College, Dublin.

RICE, JAMES. (1895–96).
1894. Entrance Exhibition, St. John's College, Cambridge.

REID, D. D.
       Scholarship in History, New College, Oxford.
1896. First Class in Modern History Class List, University of Oxford.

TABLE XI.—BENEFACTORS of QUEEN'S COLLEGE, BELFAST, since its Foundation in 1845.

A.D.

1847. Presented by Charles Davis, Esq., a large oil painting of the Assassination of Peter the Martyr, by Atkins, being a copy of the original painting by Titian.

—— Presented by Professor Craik, a portrait of Confucius.

1851. The Governors of the Armagh Observatory, with the sanction of Her Majesty, transferred to the College the Transit Instrument and Astronomical Clock which were formerly in the Observatory at Kew.

The Lords of the Admiralty, on the recommendation of the Astronomer Royal of England, acceded to an application from Professor Wilson for transferring to the College a Mural Circle by Jones, which had been in use at the Cape of Good Hope.

For the reception of these instruments an Observatory was erected on the College grounds, the expense having been defrayed by subscription.

1851. Presented by W. P. Wilson, Esq., M.A., former Professor of Mathematics in the College, a Bust of Sir Isaac Newton.

1853. Presented by Robert H. Lynn, Esq., London, an oil portrait of James the First of England when a child, an oil portrait of James Carolus, and an oil portrait of John Milton.

1860. An oil portrait of Hugh Carlisle, M.D., former Professor of Anatomy and Physiology in the College; presented by the subscribers.

1864. Given by R. M. Wilson, Esq., an Exhibition of Twenty Pounds to be conferred annually upon one or more of the most deserving unsuccessful candidates for a Scholarship of the First Year.

This Exhibition was awarded for eleven years.

1864. Given by the Royal Academical Institution, Belfast, two Exhibitions of Five Pounds each, to be conferred annually upon students from that Institution who have taken the highest places in the Literary and Science Divisions, at the Examination for Scholarships of the First Year.

1866. Given by John Charters, Esq., an Exhibition, value Fifteen Pounds, and two Exhibitions, value Ten Pounds each, in the Literary Division of the Faculty of Arts; also one Exhibition, value Fifteen Pounds, and two, value Ten Pounds each, in the Science Division of the Faculty of Arts, to be called the "Charters' Exhibitions," and to be annually awarded during ten years, at the Examinations for the Literary and Scientific Scholarships of the first year, to students who, during at least one year previous to their entrance into college, have been in continuous attendance at the Royal Academical Institution, and who have attained the standard of excellence required at the Junior Scholarship Examinations. Also, an Exhibition, value Fifty Pounds, tenable for one year, to be called the "Charters' Medical Exhibition," to be annually awarded during ten years, in connexion with the Belfast School of Medicine, by the Trustees of the "Charters' Educational Fund."

—— An oil portrait of William Burden, M.D., former Professor of Midwifery in the College; presented by the subscribers.

1868. Bequeathed by Robert Sullivan, Esq., LL.D., Barrister-at-Law, the sum of Four Thousand Pounds for the endowment of Three Scholarships in Queen's College, Belfast, to be called the Sullivan Scholarships, two of them to be restricted to candidates who shall have acted as Teachers or Assistant Teachers in Irish National Schools for at least two years, and one of them to candidates who shall have been educated in the Royal Academical Institution, Belfast, for at least three years.

These Scholarships are tenable for three years.

A.D.

1869. Given by William Coates, Esq., a prize, value Thirty Pounds, to be called "The Coates Prize," and to be awarded in the Department of Engineering to the best candidates in a set of Examinations, to be held in the Third term of each Session, and to comprise :—

   1. Civil and Mechanical Engineering.

   2. Office and Field Work, including Geometrical Drawing and Surveying, Levelling and Measuring, together with any two of the following subjects :—

   3. Natural Philosophy applied.

   4. Analytical Chemistry.

   5. Geology.

   6. Mathematics, including specially the elementary principles of the Differential Calculus.

Competition for this Prize in each Session to be open to all persons who are at the time, or were in the preceding year, Students of Engineering in Queen's College, Belfast, going through the Third Session of their Engineering Course, in regular order, or going through the Session which, under the sanction of the Council, in special cases shall stand instead of a Third Session of the Queen's College Engineering Course.

This prize was awarded for four years.

1869. A Bust of the Rev. P. Shuldham Henry, D.D., late President of the College, presented by the Professors and other subscribers.

1871. An oil portrait of George L. Craik, LL.D., former Professor of History and English Literature in the College, and also a photograph group of some of the Professors; presented by Messrs. Marcus Ward & Co.

1871. Bequeathed by John Porter, Esq., the sum of Three Thousand One Hundred and Ten Pounds Eight Shillings and Four Pence for the endowment of Two Scholarships in Queen's College, Belfast, to be called "The Porter Scholarships." These scholarships are each of the annual value of Fifty Pounds, and are tenable for two years. They are open to undergraduates of not less than two years' standing.

1873. A deed was executed by William Danville, Esq., establishing the "Sorella Trust."

This deed, which also provides funds for other educational purposes not connected with the College, endows two Studentships in Queen's College, Belfast, to be called "The Danville Studentships." These studentships are open to any person who is recognised by the Council or other Governing body of Queen's College, Belfast, as a student of three or more years' standing in any Faculty, provided that the last of the three or more years which give such standing, has been spent in Queen's College, Belfast, and has been the year preceding, or the year but one preceding the examination.

They are given, one, for the encouragement of the study of Mathematical and Physical Sciences, the other, for the encouragement of the study of Natural Science, in alternate years. Each person obtaining a Studentship receives £45 for the first year, and £100 for the second year.

1873. Given by the Widow and Children of the late John Robinson M'Clean, Esq., Civil Engineer, London, through the hands of the Rev. P. S. Henry, D.D., President, the sum of Five Hundred Pounds, to be expended in the purchase of Scientific works for the Library of Queen's College, Belfast.

Anno.

1874. Given by the Methodist College, Belfast, one Exhibition, value Ten
Pounds, to be awarded annually to the highest answerer among students
from the Methodist College who have obtained Literary Scholarships of
the first year in Queen's College, Belfast; and another Exhibition, also
value Ten Pounds, to the highest answerer among students from the
Methodist College, who have obtained Science Scholarships of the First
Year in the same College.

1876. Given by the Reverend Arthur Hercules Pakenham, for the endowment
of two Scholarships in Queen's College, Belfast, one to be called the
" Sir Hercules Pakenham Scholarship," and the other the "Emily Lady
Pakenham Scholarship," the sum of One Thousand Pounds, invested in
five bonds of £100 each of the Moscow Jaroslaw Railway Company, and
five bonds of £100 each of the Charkoff Azov Railway Company.

These Scholarships are given in alternate years, are each tenable for
two years, and are open to all students under 20 years of age, matriculated
or non-matriculated, on their first entrance into the College.

1877. Given by an anonymous donor, Ten Pounds, to provide for an Entrance
Prize of Five Pounds, to be awarded for proficiency in French.

This prize was awarded for two years.

1878. An oil portrait of Alexander Gordon, M.D., former Professor of Surgery
in the College; presented by the subscribers.

1880. The subscribers to a testimonial given to Dr. MacDouall on his retire-
ment from the Professorship of Greek, presented to the College, in
addition to a portrait of Dr. MacDouall now placed in the Examination
Hall, a collection of Classical and Oriental Works of the value of
£275, selected from the library of Dr. MacDouall, to form the nucleus
of a department of the Library to be called " The MacDouall Library."

1881. The sum of One Thousand Seven Hundred and Ninety-two Pounds Seven
Shillings was raised by public subscription, for the establishment of a
Scholarship to commemorate the distinguished services, rendered to this
College and to Chemical Science, by Dr. Thomas Andrews, F.R.S., the late
Vice-President.

At the same time a full-length Oil Portrait of Dr. Andrews was placed
in the Examination Hall.

1881. The sum of Eight Hundred and Seventy-five Pounds Six Shillings, in
New Three per Cent. Government Stock, being a portion of the bequest
of the late Lord Blayney, was transferred to this College by the
Queen's University.

1882. A Medal, to be awarded annually, was founded with a portion of the
residue of the Peel Fund of the late Queen's University.

1882. An Oil Portrait of William Nesbitt, M.A., former Professor of Latin
in the College; presented by the Subscribers.

1889. Bequeathed by John M'Kane, Esq., LL.D., Barrister-at-Law, former
Professor of English Law in the College, a Gold Medal to be awarded
annually for answering in Jurisprudence and Political Economy.

1889. An Oil Portrait of the Rev. J. Leslie Porter, D.D., LL.D., late President
of the College; presented by the President and Professors.

1890. An Oil Portrait of John Purser, LL.D., Professor of Mathematics in the
College; presented by his former students.

1891. Given by Her Majesty's Commissioners of the Exhibition of 1851 the
nomination to a Scholarship of the value of £150 per annum, tenable for
two, or, under special conditions, for three years, and limited to those
branches of Science (such as Physics, Mechanics, and Chemistry), the
extension of which is specially important for our national industries.

1893. Given by Her Majesty's Commissioners of the Exhibition of 1851 the
nomination to a Scholarship of the value of £150 per annum, tenable for
two, or, under special conditions, for three years, as above.

Anno.

1893. Founded by the Trustees of the Sorella Trust the "Dunville Chair of Physiology."

1894. An Oil Portrait of Peter Redfern, M.D., Professor of Anatomy and Physiology 1860-93; presented by the Subscribers.

1894. Subscribed, and raised by a Fancy Fair about £3,000 for the erection of a College Union.

1895. Given by Her Majesty's Commissioners of the Exhibition of 1851 the nomination to a Scholarship of the value of £150 per annum, tenable for two, or, under special conditions, for three years, as above.

1895. An Oil Painting of James MacAdam, Esq., the first Librarian of the College, presented by Miss MacAdam.

1896. Given by the Trustees of the Sorella Trust the sum of £100 for the purchase of apparatus for the department of Physiology.

DONATIONS to the LIBRARY, 1895-96.

Donations.	Presented.
R. R. Sharpe: London and the Kingdom. Vol. III.	By the Corporation of the City of London.
Proceedings and Transactions of the Royal Society of Canada.	By the President and Council.
H. D. Darbishire: Reliquiæ Philologicæ.	By Mr. and Mrs. Darbishire.
Vida de Rufino Cuervo, 2 vols.	By his sons, Angel and Rufino José.
Opere di Galileo Galilei, Edizione Nazionale. Vol. V.	By the Minister of Public Instruction, Rome.
Report of University College, Bristol.	By the Council.
Supplement to the Catalogue of the Library of King's College, Aberdeen.	By the University Court.
Reports of the Middlesex Hospital for 1890 and 1894.	By the Governors.
E. Suervestre: Un Philosophe sous les Toits.	By Messrs. Macmillan.
F. H. Stevens: Elementary Mensuration.	By Messrs. Macmillan.
Cosm, by Historicus.	By Mr. Cadbury.
Mittheilungen der Medizinischen Fakultät der Japanischen Universität zu Tokio.	By the Medical Faculty of Tokio.
Eustace H. Miles: The Middle Voice.	By the Author.
Report of the Superintendent of Public Instruction for the City of Brooklyn.	By the Superintendent, Mr. W. H. Maxwell.
Nihongi: Chronicles of Japan, translated by W. G. Aston, C.M.G.	By the Translator.
The Jubilee Meeting of the Chemico-Agricultural Society of Ulster.	By Professor Hodges.
Tantallan Castle, the Story of the Castle and the Ship.	By Messrs. Donald Currie and Co.
Christopher J. Street: Immortal Life. ——— Jesus the Prophet.	} By the Author.
Fifty-five Reports and Parts of Periodicals on Agricultural Subjects.	By Professor Hodges.
Fifty Volumes on Metaphysical Subjects.	By Professor Park.

The following Institutions have continued to present their publications:—

    The Royal Irish Academy.
    The British Museum.
    The Government of India.
          „   „   China (Customs).
          „   „   Canada (Geological Survey).
          „   „   Norway (North Pole Expedition).
    The Cambridge Philosophical Society.
    The Philosophical Society, Birmingham.
    The Institute of Civil Engineers.
    The South Kensington Museum.
    The Smithsonian Institution.
    The Bureau of Education, Washington.

The following Universities and Colleges presented their Calendars:—

    The University of Aberdeen.
        „   „   Edinburgh.
        „   „   Glasgow.
        „   „   St. Andrews.
        „   „   Durham.
    Victoria University.
    Royal University of Ireland.
    The University of California.
    Owens College, Manchester.
    Queen's College, Birmingham.
    Mason College, Birmingham.
    University College, Bristol.
    The Yorkshire College, Leeds.
    University College, Dundee.
    Anderson's College, Glasgow.
    The College of Medicine, Newcastle-on-Tyne.
    Queen's College, Cork.
    Queen's College, Galway.

DONATIONS TO THE NATURAL HISTORY MUSEUM

A considerable number of donations have been received from friends, among which the following may be mentioned:—

Bear and Fox, presented by David Walker, esq., M.D., a former student of the College.

Collection of Shells presented by Mrs. M'Gee, widow of the late Dr. M'Gee.

Casts and specimens of extinct animals, presented by the Earl of Enniskillen.

Five very rare Birds from Yarkand, presented by Dr. Scully, Indian Medical Service.

Collections of Japanese Birds, prepared and presented by Dr. S. Campbell, Fleet Surgeon, R.N.

Collections of Animals, chiefly Marine, from the East Coast of Africa and Zulu Archipelago, presented by Lieut. Dixon, R.N.

Miscellaneous specimens, presented by Staff-Surgeon W. Anderson, R.N., a former student of the College.

Large collection of Indian birds, some of considerable rarity, presented on various occasions by Dr. Cunningham, Professor of Physiology, Medical College, Calcutta.

Specimens of North American birds and Irish fishes, presented by G. D. Ogilby, esq., a student of the College.

Collection of Animals and Minerals from Australia, presented by Edward Leslie Pooler, esq., M.D., a former student of the College.

Collection of Animals from the New Hebrides, &c., presented by James Dunlop, esq., M.D., Surgeon R.N., a former student of the College.

Collection of Animals from Sumatra, presented by John B. Graham, esq., M.D., a former student of the College.

Collection of Birds from the Himalayas, presented by Alexander Porter, esq., M.D., Brigade Surgeon, H.M. Indian Army, a former student of the College.

Collection of Reptiles from South Australia, presented by Edward Leslie Pooler, esq., M.D., a former student of the College.

Very fine specimen of *Goliathus Drurpi* from West Africa, presented by R. J. M'Keown, esq., M.D., a former student of the College.

Two fine specimens of the remarkable New Zealand Lizard, *Sphenodon*, presented by James Young, esq., M.D., New Zealand, a former student of the College.

A fine specimen of *Manis longicaudata*, and a queen Termite or White Ant, presented by Captain R. A. L. Irvine.

A collection of dried plants and other objects from Ulster, presented by Hugh Hyndman, esq., LL.D., a former student of the College.

DONATIONS TO THE MEDICAL MUSEUMS.

A beautiful series of microscopical preparations, showing the texture of many organs of the body, was presented by Dr. Thiersch, of Leipsic, to Dr. Redfern, Professor of Anatomy, and by him generously handed over to the College.

A series of 59 slides, containing embryological sections prepared under his personal superintendence, was presented by Professor Kölliker to Dr. Redfern, and by him to the College.

A fine collection of over 200 vesical calculi removed by surgical operation in India by Surgeon-Major J. A. Cunningham, Indian Medical Service, a former student of the College, and presented by him.

A very large collection of specimens, formerly in Minto House, Edinburgh, presented by Professor Symington.

TABLE XII.—ACCOUNT OF THE RECEIPTS AND EXPENDITURE OF

RECEIPTS.	£ s. d.		
Balance on 1st April, 1896, viz. :—			
General Account, ...	£906 0 1		
Endowment Accounts, ...	245 12 6		
Library Deposits, ...	410 0 0		
		1,561 12 9	
Grant charged on Consolidated Fund, ...	£1,800 0 0		
Less Income Tax, ...	170 0 0		
		1,630 0 0	
Annual Grants of Parliament, viz. :—			
In Aid of Expenses of Maintenance, ...		1,600 0 0	
In Aid of Augmentation of Professors' Salaries, . .	£150 0 0		
Less Income Tax, ...	0 0 0		
		145 0 0	
Private Endowment of The Dunville Chair of Physiology.	£240 0 0		
Less Income Tax, ...	0 0 0		
		232 0 0	
Professors' Class Fees, ...		1,429 10 0	
Lecturers' Class Fees, ...		149 0 0	
College Fees, viz. :—			
461 at 10s., ...	£230 10 0		
1 at 6s., for use of Library, ...	0 6 0		
Calendars sold, ...	1 1 0		
		231 7 0	
Dividends on Government Stock, ...		97 4 10	
Endowments, ...		911 0 5	
Library Deposits, ...		110 0 0	
		£11,279 11 7	

THE COLLEGE IN THE YEAR ENDING 31st MARCH, 1896.

PAYMENTS.   £ s. d.

Salaries, &c., paid out of Permanent Grant:—			
President, Professors, and Officers,	£4,660 0 0		
Less Income Tax,	204 16 4		
		£4,639 0 0	
Scholarships and Prizes,		1,419 11 0	
Minor Officers and Servants,	£400 0 0		
Less Income Tax,	9 6 8		
		400 14 0	
Lecturer in Pathology,		50 0 0	
			4,720 14 5
Salaries of Professors paid out of Special Grant,	£140 0 0		
Less Income Tax,	9 0 0		
		145 0 0	
Library:—			
Ancient and Modern Languages,	£60 0 0		
Mathematical and Physical Sciences,	38 6 11		
Natural Sciences,	44 14 3		
Engineering,	9 19 4		
Medical Sciences,	77 10 7		
Mental and Legal Sciences,	33 4 8		
General Department,	64 4 0		
Binding,	64 11 0		
Cataloguing,	170 0 0		
		643 9 10	
Laboratories:—			
Chemical Laboratory,	553 1 3		
Physical Cabinet,	64 14 6		
Engineering,	31 11 1		
Medical Faculty,	343 13 7		
		710 10 0	
Museums,		77 15 5	
Printing, Stationery, and Advertising,		167 19 11	
Heating and Lighting,		976 7 10	
Botanic Garden and College Grounds,		95 17 0	
Miscellaneous, viz.:—			
Porters' Clothing,	437 3 0		
Water Supply,	96 3 0		
To supplement Porters' Salaries,	61 17 4		
Incidental Expenses,	210 9 9		
		857 17 1	
Practical Pharmacy Department, Special,		4 15 5	
Pathological Department, Special,		17 14 4	
Equipment of New Chemical Laboratory, Special,		49 7 0	
Fittings for new Physiological and Pathological Laboratories, Special,		41 4 5	
Dunville Professor of Physiology,		500 0 0	
Professors' Class Fees,		2,420 16 0	
Lecturers' Class Fees,		149 0 0	
Made-up rents,		900 0 7	
Library Deposits,		114 0 0	
Balance on 31st March, 1896, viz.:—			
General Account,	£554 0 1		
Endowment Accounts,	173 11 10		
Library Deposits,	418 0 0		
		1,147 0 11	
		£14,572 11 7